10-Minute
CUISINE

10-Minute
CUISINE

HENRIETTA GREEN AND
MARIE-PIERRE MOINE

A FIRESIDE BOOK
PUBLISHED BY SIMON & SCHUSTER INC.
NEW YORK LONDON TORONTO SYDNEY TOKYO SINGAPORE

DEDICATION

To Auden of Portobello and Dickie
of Amboise – our faithful friends

Throughout the book the half-plate
symbol has been used to
indicate a starter portion, and the
full-plate symbol ● to denote a
main-course portion. Recipes are
for 4 people, unless otherwise
stated.

First published in 1991 by
Conran Octopus Limited
37 Shelton Street, London WC2H 9HN

Text copyright (c) Henrietta Green &
Marie-Pierre Moine

F **Fireside**
Simon & Schuster Building
Rockefeller Center
1230 Avenue of the Americas
New York, New York 10020

FIRESIDE and colophon
are registered trademarks
of Simon & Schuster Inc.

Library of Congress
Cataloging in Publication Data
Available upon request

Typeset by Servis Filmsetting Limited
Printed and bound by Kim Hup Lee Printing
Co PTE Ltd, Singapore

Contents

Introduction

10-minute Cuisine *is the result of our love of good food and lack of time to prepare it. We have written the book for everyone who, like us, can cook and enjoys doing so but has neither the time – nor, perhaps, the inclination – to spend a lot of time in the kitchen.*

We had real problems in the past, as we liked to eat fresh food but were both very busy. We tried microwave cooking and found that, as a basic way of cooking, it just was not for us. We then tried cooked-chilled food and, frankly, the dishes were boring, over-priced, under-seasoned, and laden with preservatives. In desperation, we evolved our own ways of cooking good fresh food very fast.

We turned ourselves into cooks "à la 10-minute" – the domestic equivalent of short-order cooks. In our case, the back-up brigade consisted of the right ingredients, the right techniques, and the right equipment – including a food processor, which has proved invaluable!

In 10 minutes there is only so much you can achieve. Subtlety is out; but intense flavors, clean sharp tastes and firm textures more than make up for it. The idea is to turn the lack of time into an advantage.

If you think this sounds daunting and involves too much frantic activity, you could not be more wrong. 10-minute cuisine is fun, brisk, and enjoyable. The secret lies in concentrating on quality produce; preparing it quickly and effectively; and in using the most suitable equipment. We have cut out all unnecessary details – from fiddly preparations to fancy garnishes – and pared the process down to the essentials.

We may be stingy with our time but we are certainly liberal with our food: a generous table needs no trimmings. We do not go for elaborate presentation or individual plating – everyone helps themselves straight from the pot and from large bowls and dishes.

10-minute Cuisine *means the busiest person can enjoy cooking – and even entertaining! We love our fast food: it is bold, vibrant, and gutsy; and the dishes are full of flavor and freshness. We hope you will have as much fun cooking and eating it as we do.*

Ingredients

10-minute cuisine is bold, decisive, and very quick. Our fast approach relies essentially on the quality of the ingredients we use and is unlike most traditional methods of cooking, where flavors are gently nursed and coaxed until they are developed to the full.

Since we have no time for long braises or slow simmers, what we are aiming for is the fastest possible release of the taste of ingredients. For this reason we always use the best – the freshest and most intensely flavored – produce.

Obviously, this great burst of taste can only be achieved if the ingredients are good enough to start with. First of all they must be fresh. Consequently we are great believers in the old-fashioned way of shopping "little and often," so that the food we use never sits around for long. This practice includes staples such as eggs, butter, cheese, and the spices in our kitchen cabinets, as well as the more obvious vegetables, fruit, meat, and fish. Everything must be in top condition.

We also try to buy produce in season. Not only is it better value, but very often it is at its peak of flavor as it has ripened at its natural pace. What we save on buying seasonally, we may spend on convenience. This sometimes takes the form of pre-washed and cut vegetables, pre-packed and selected salad leaves, boned and trimmed meat or skinned and filleted fish. They cost more, but they do save precious time.

One of our many extravagances – for which we offer no apology – is the liberal use of fresh herbs. With their pungent flavors, they are invaluable for fast and bold cooking and are far more effective than dried herbs. We also use extra-virgin olive oil – not just for dressings, but also for cooking – and we assume you will, too. The wine we cook with is the wine we drink. So-called "cooking" wines can spoil the flavor of a sauce. You will find that in many of our recipes we do not specify which wine to use – but we do assume that it will be on the dry side.

We do, however, specify wine vinegar or cider vinegar, as – in our opinion – their contribution is unique. Any other vinegars – malt in particular – are so sharp that they could destroy the dish. Both of us only ever use sea salt, because you need less of it and it blends better with – and brings out more rapidly – the flavor of the food. For the same reasons we only ever use freshly ground black pepper.

In an ideal world we would buy only organic produce, as the flavor is usually stronger. Unfortunately, the price is often prohibitive so we have to compromise. One thing we insist on is unwaxed citrus fruit, particularly if we are using the zest. "Waxing" is a euphemism for coating fruit with a nasty cocktail of chemicals, particularly anti-fungal preparations (which stop the fruit from getting moldy but are neither healthy nor flavorsome). If you have to use waxed fruit, scrub the skin with a stiff brush several times in warm soapy water, rinse well and rub dry.

On the vexed question of eggs, as we occasionally use lightly cooked – or even raw – eggs, we try to buy them from trusted sources which guarantee them to be safe.

In fact, we generally try to buy from smaller specialty producers or specialist shops which assure us of good service, personal attention, and the freshness and quality of their produce. This makes shopping much more satisfying. If you are tempted to pursue our style of cooking, perhaps you too should build up your own network of suppliers.

Since, more often than not, the occasions on which you have to cook in 10 minutes are precisely those when you are most pushed for time, it helps to keep a few basics in the kitchen.

Obviously we always have staples such as:

IN THE PANTRY:

GARLIC
SEA SALT
BLACK PEPPERCORNS
SUGAR

which get turned over pretty quickly. Although we have already said we prefer to buy food when and if we need it, we list below items which will keep for a while and are frequently very useful:

IN THE REFRIGERATOR:

EGGS
BUTTER
MILK
2 OR 3 LEMONS AND ORANGES
BUNCH OF SCALLIONS
BOTTLE OF DRY WHITE WINE
SOME BACON
LARGE CARTON OF YOGURT
CHUNK OF PARMESAN
DRY HARD CIDER

IN THE FREEZER:

STICKS OF BUTTER
CHICKEN/ VEGETABLE/ FISH
  STOCK (EITHER HOMEMADE,
  WHEN WE ARE LESS PUSHED
  FOR TIME, OR BOUGHT)
CARTON OF GOOD QUALITY
  VANILLA ICE-CREAM
PACKAGE OF LEAF SPINACH
PACKAGE OF SMALL GREEN
  PEAS
LOAF OF GOOD BREAD

ON THE WINDOW SILL:

Since we do use such a lot of different fresh herbs, we try to grow as many as we can on our window sills. Not only does this save money, time, and effort, it is also great fun.

Most big supermarket chains now sell plastic containers of growing herbs: parsley, cilantro, chives, thyme, basil, chervil, sage, tarragon, and mint. These cost no more than a tiny package of cut fresh herbs, but they last much longer and we highly recommend them.

We make an exception for flat-leaf parsley, which we prefer to the moss-curled variety. As we are constantly using it in vast quantities, we buy it in bunches. These we keep in the kitchen: either in a pitcher of water on a shady window ledge or in the refrigerator, wrapped in damp newspaper inside a plastic bag.

IN THE KITCHEN CABINETS:

10-MINUTE RICE
DRIED PASTA AND/OR NOODLES
EXTRA-VIRGIN OLIVE OIL
PEANUT OR SUNFLOWER OIL
WALNUT OIL AND/OR HAZELNUT
    OIL
RED AND WHITE WINE VINEGAR
CIDER VINEGAR
½ BOTTLE OF DRY SHERRY
SOY SAUCE
MUSTARD POWDER
WORCESTERSHIRE SAUCE
GOOD MUSTARD (KEEP IN
    REFRIGERATOR ONCE
    OPENED)
ANCHOVY FILLETS
ANCHOVY ESSENCE
TAHINI
TABASCO
HARISSA OR CHILI SAUCE
CORIANDER SEEDS
NUTMEG
PAPRIKA
CUMIN
SMALL DRIED CHILIS
CAPERS
HONEY
RED CURRANT JELLY
MARMALADE
BLANCHED ALMONDS
SEEDLESS RAISINS
PINE NUTS/HAZELNUTS/
    WALNUTS
POPPY SEEDS/SUNFLOWER
    SEEDS
CABINET SAUCES (SEE PAGE 18)
CANS (SEE PAGE 20)

INGREDIENTS

KITCHEN CABINET SAUCES

The 10-minute cook can prepare these invaluable sauces when there is time, then store and use them later to give added interest and extra flavor to a wide variety of dishes. We usually have at least a couple on the go at any one time. They are a boon when there is no time for shopping or an unexpected meal to cook: they are great for perking up anything from pasta to a dessert, and can be used to make a quick paste-paint or even a compound butter.

1 SUN-DRIED TOMATOES IN OIL

You can buy sun-dried tomatoes in oil, but they are expensive and a little bland. We prefer to buy them dried, and bottle them in oil ourselves. We are indebted to Anna Del Conte, whose recipe from *Secrets from an Italian Kitchen* produces a particularly deep and pungent flavor.

Cover 1 pound sun-dried tomatoes with a mixture of equal parts boiling water and wine vinegar and let them soak 1 hour. Turn them over and leave them a further 1½ hours. Drain and pat dry with paper towels.

In a clean glass jar, place the tomatoes in layers, sprinkling each layer with handfuls of snipped oregano and chopped garlic. Pour in extra-virgin olive oil to cover (about 1¼ cups), making sure there is no air trapped between the layers by sliding a narrow spatula down the side of the jar. Let steep until required.

2 LABNA BALLS IN OIL

Again, you can buy labna balls in oil from Greek and Turkish grocers. However, we generally prefer the flavor of homemade ones. The method we use comes from Peter Graham's *Classic Cheese Cookery*, but the flavorings are our own.

Pour 2½ cups of Greek-style thick, strained cows' milk yogurt into a colander lined with several layers of damp cheesecloth. Let stand in a bowl overnight in a cool place.

Next day, tie the cheesecloth into a bundle and suspend this over the bowl about another 24 hours to extract more whey and to make the labna even firmer.

Untie the cheesecloth and roll the labna a little at a time into small balls, 1½ inches in diameter, between the palms of your hands. Place the balls in layers in a clean glass jar, sprinkling each layer with equal parts of a mixture of the zest of 1 orange and 1 lemon, 1 snipped scallion, a handful of snipped flat-leaf parsley and 2 crushed black peppercorns. Pour in 1 tablespoon of orange flower water and then cover with extra-virgin olive oil.

3 CHILI OIL

We find flavored oils extremely useful when cooking in 10 minutes. There are endless variations, but because of our approach we go for strong flavors with plenty of punch – Chili Oil is one of the most versatile.

To prepare it, simply take a handful of small chili peppers (remember – the smaller and thinner the chili, the hotter it is), prick them all several times with a needle and put them in a clean jar covered with extra-virgin olive oil. Let steep at least 1 week.

It is less fiery than most commercial chili oils, but still use it sparingly!

4 ROASTED GARLIC IN OIL

Heat the oven to 350°F. Paint 3 heads of garlic lightly with olive oil and sprinkle them with sea salt. Bake them on a baking sheet in the oven for 45 minutes. Let cool, then put them in a clean jar and pour in enough extra-virgin olive oil to cover.

To use: break off as many cloves as you need, and squeeze them to extract the pulp.

5 TAPENADE

Pit 1 cup ripe olives. In the food processor, whizz them along with 3 garlic cloves, a handful of mixed thyme, rosemary, and oregano, a dash each of Tabasco and anchovy essence and a pinch of ground cilantro. Trickle in 6 tablespoons of extra-virgin olive oil and whizz again. Spoon into a clean bowl or jar, cover and chill until needed. Tapenade will keep up to 1 month in the refrigerator.

6 PRUNES IN BRANDY

Take 1 pound large prunes and pack them loosely into a clean glass jar. Break up a small stick of cinnamon, add the pieces to the jar along with the zest of 1 orange. Make a light syrup by boiling $\frac{3}{4}$ cup sugar with $\frac{2}{3}$ cup water 5 minutes. Let cool and pour into the jar. Fill jar with brandy, seal the jar and give it a thorough shake. Leave at least 1 week.

7 RAISINS IN SCOTCH

Take $\frac{1}{2}$ pound ($1\frac{1}{2}$ cups) seedless raisins and pack them loosely in a clean glass jar. Pour in enough scotch to cover and let soak 1 or 2 days. Add extra scotch if required.

12 THINGS TO DO WITH CANS

All our recipes are based on fresh ingredients because that is how we like to cook. However, quite a few good things can come out of cans. Here are our "Top 12," and we suggest that you always have some of the following cans in stock.

CLAMS (IN BRINE)
TUNA (IN OIL)
ARTICHOKE HEARTS
CANNELLINI BEANS
CHICKPEAS (GARBANZOS)
FLAGEOLETS OR LIMA BEANS
PETIT POIS
WHOLE KERNEL CORN
PIMIENTOES
TOMATOES
CHESTNUT PURÉE
   (SWEETENED)
BLACK CHERRIES (IN SYRUP)

1 CREAMY CORN SOUP

Tip the contents of a large can of whole kernel corn into a saucepan. Half fill the can with water and then fill with milk. Pour this into the pan, add a dash of white wine and a few sprigs of thyme, and bring to a simmer. Stir in 1 or 2 tablespoons of cream and season to taste with sea salt and freshly ground black pepper.

2 ARTICHOKE AND RIPE OLIVE SAUCE

Drain the contents of a medium can of artichoke hearts. Roughly chop the hearts and put them in a bowl. Snip in some parsley and pitted ripe olives and stir in a little olive oil. Season with sea salt and freshly ground black pepper. Mix into cooked and drained pasta (see No-cook Sauces for Pasta on page 45).

3 PIMIENTO AND TUNA SAUCE

Drain the contents of a medium can of pimientoes and a small can of tuna. Roughly chop the pimientoes and mix with the tuna. Snip in some chives and stir in a little olive oil. Season with sea salt and freshly ground black pepper. Mix into cooked and drained pasta (see No-cook Sauces for Pasta on page 45).

4 CLAM AND TOMATO SAUCE

Bring to a boil the contents of a medium can of tomatoes with a minced garlic clove, a pinch of sugar, and some snipped oregano and thyme. Simmer 3 minutes until slightly thickened. Add a dash each of white wine and olive oil and simmer another 1 minute. Drain the contents of a small can of clams and tip the clams into the sauce. Stir gently until heated through and season to taste with sea salt and freshly ground black pepper. This is an ideal hot pasta sauce (see pages 44-7).

5 PEA AND CREAM SAUCE

Drain the contents of a medium can of petits pois. Tip the peas into a saucepan along with about $\frac{1}{2}$ cup of light cream and bring to a simmer. Season to taste with sea salt and freshly ground black pepper. Pour over cooked and drained pasta (see pages 44–7). Snip over a few lettuce leaves.

6 INSTANT HUMMUS

Whizz together the drained contents of a medium can of chickpeas (garbanzos), a couple of garlic cloves, some olive oil, a little tahini, and the juice of $\frac{1}{2}$ a lemon. Season to taste with sea salt and freshly ground black pepper. Sprinkle with a little paprika, snip over some cilantro. Serve with ripe olives.

7 BEAN AND TUNA SALAD

Drain and rinse the contents of a medium can of cannellini beans and drain a small can of tuna. Mix them together, snip over 1 or 2 scallions and some parsley. Stir in a little olive oil, the juice of $\frac{1}{2}$ a lemon, and season to taste with sea salt and freshly ground black pepper.

8 CHICKPEA AND TAHINI SALAD

Drain and rinse the contents of a medium can of chickpeas (garbanzos). Stir in a little tahini, a dash of wine vinegar, a couple of chopped tomatoes, and snip over some mint. Season to taste with sea salt and freshly ground black pepper.

9 SWEET RED PEPPER SAUCE

Whizz the drained contents of a small can of pimientoes with a garlic clove and a little olive oil. Season to taste with sea salt and freshly ground black pepper. Ideal with grilled chicken or hamburgers.

10 FLAGEOLETS

Drain and rinse the contents of a medium can of flageolets or lima beans. Melt a pat of butter in a sauté pan and add the beans. Snip in a couple of scallions and add a dash of white wine. Heat through gently and season to taste with sea salt and freshly ground black pepper. Ideal with broiled lamb chops.

11 CHESTNUT PURÉE WITH YOGURT

Whizz the contents of a small can of chestnut purée with 1-$1\frac{1}{4}$ cups of thick set (Swiss-style) yogurt, the zest and juice of $\frac{1}{2}$ an orange, and a dash of brandy. Sweeten to taste with honey or sugar.

12 CHERRY SAUCE

Tip the contents of a small can of black cherries into a saucepan. Add a generous dash of Kirsch and heat gently. Ideal with ice-cream.

Equipment

There is no getting around the fact that in order to cook fresh food very fast, you need to have a relatively well-equipped kitchen and, to save time, the right appliances for the job. We are assuming that the reader already has a basic batterie de cuisine, *which includes a few good quality utensils and gadgets such as a sieve, a colander, a couple of whisks, various wooden spoons, and a couple of spatulas.*

What we do not intend is that anyone spend money on unnecessary high-tech clutter, or the latest multi-function microwave oven. In fact, one of us does not even own a microwave and the other only uses it to reheat coffee.

However, there is one major piece of equipment we feel is worth investing in, and that is a food processor. We are addicted to our food processors, because they do everything very fast and very efficiently. We both own a Magimix Système Cuisine 3000, which has an additional smaller bowl for small quantities of sauces and purées. We have found that the more boldly and frequently you use a food processor, the more satisfactory the results. Without them, frankly, we could never even have contemplated writing this book, as most of the recipes would have taken three times as long.

A number of other tools are essential for our 10-minute cuisine. These are as follows:

UTENSILS & GADGETS

KNIVES

Good knives are invaluable, as our approach to cooking involves fast preparation as much as fast cooking. We suggest you use whatever shape and size of knife you are most comfortable with. It goes without saying that you must keep your knives sharp and within easy reach.

ZESTER

You will need a zester for zesting fruit (see page 31). This is a useful little utensil with tiny holes at the end of its blade which shave off thin strips of peel without lifting off any of the bitter pith just underneath. It is a boon when every second counts and you have no time to blanch the zest.

SCISSORS

Scissors are important as we use them for snipping (see page 30). There are a number of specialist kitchen scissors available – from fish scissors to poultry shears – but we are more than happy with the all-purpose ones providing you keep them very sharp. For reasons of hygiene, you really ought to have at least 3 pairs: one for herbs and vegetables; one for cooked meat and fish; and a third strictly reserved for raw meat and fish. A good idea is to buy each pair with a different color handle and this, in turn, could be color-coordinated with one of 3 corresponding chopping boards.

BRUSH

For paste-painting (see page 31) a brush is essential. Choose a strong well-made brush which can cope with applying a heavy paste without bending or shedding bristles. Whether it is flat or round is immaterial, but if there is a large surface to paint, a wide brush will obviously do the job much quicker. Nylon bristles are fine, but bear in mind that they may melt when used on a hot surface.

SALAD DRYER

When it comes to washing salads, time can be saved by using a salad spin-dryer. This relatively inexpensive gadget is a sophisticated version of the old-fashioned salad shaker and utilizes the principle of centrifugal force. The washed leaves are put in an inner rotating basket and as it spins, the water is driven out to the outer bowl. For the little they cost, we think they are an excellent investment.

WOK & SCOOP

Since we stir-fry a lot (see page 32), a wok and wok scoop are important. Our woks are the "cheap and cheerful" variety acquired at the nearest Chinese supermarket and are replaced relatively frequently as they quickly rust or discolor. As neither of us is particularly skilled or strong-wristed, we prefer the classic single-handled model which is far easier to manipulate.

SAUTÉ PAN

A good sauté pan is incredibly versatile. With its deep sides, it is more flexible than a skillet and we use it to sauté, steam-boil (see page 32), and poach – all vital methods for cooking fresh food fast. We recommend investing in a good-quality heavy-based pan, made from copper or teflon (or any other non-stick material). As we use our sauté pan for steam-boiling, it should also have a tight-fitting lid.

For sautéing small amounts of food, and also for cooking Eggahs (see page 51), we use a 7-inch copper-based omelette pan.

PASTA PAN

We cook a lot of pasta and have both bought a proper pasta pan – ruinously expensive, but an investment we have never regretted. A pasta pan is made from stainless steel, and is deep-sided with a fitted draining basket and a tight-fitting lid. To drain the cooked pasta, all you do is lift out the basket.

APPLIANCES

An efficient cooktop is essential. We are happier with gas because the heat is instant and easier to control.

Obviously every kitchen has an oven, but we hardly ever use ours for fast cooking as – whether gas or electric – it takes too long to heat up. However, as broiling is one of our basic techniques (see page 31), a good broiler is also required. We both have oven broilers which work perfectly provided we remember to heat them up for a few minutes in advance. Lining the broiler pan with foil not only makes it easier to clean but also speeds up cooking, as it reflects the heat.

Should you not have a built-in broiler, the alternatives are a grill pan, a griddle, a built-in barbecue or an infra-red electric broiler.

A grill pan is usually made of ridged cast iron. Before use it is lightly brushed with oil to prevent the food from sticking, then it is heated on the stovetop. The surface of the food is instantly seared on contact with the hot grill pan, which is particularly good for red meat or a whole fish.

A griddle is also heated on top of the stove. Usually made from a thinner layer of cast iron, it has a flat surface and is more suitable for cooking vegetables.

The built-in electric barbecue is a great luxury but, if you can afford it, a delight to cook with. There are various models on the market which all work on the same principle: a steel container, holding lava rocks and a heating element, is set into a worktop. Once the rocks are hot, the food can be grilled either directly on them or over removable steel grids.

An infra-red electric broiler is free-standing and produces a higher temperature than most built-in oven broilers.

Techniques

10-minute Cuisine is all about preparing and cooking food very fast. In such a short time we could not be expected to use subtle or complex techniques. Very often we find that the quickest way to mix, tear, or break ingredients is to use our hands. We have evolved a number of straightforward methods which do the job with minimum fuss but maximum effect. Like our whole approach to cooking, they take no time at all to master.

WHIZZING

This is a word you will find in most of our recipes. What it means is to process food just long enough in a food processor to achieve a desired texture. The timing will vary depending on whether the item is to be roughly chopped or smoothly puréed.

To whizz efficiently, first break, slice, or snip the food into manageable pieces (the exact size will obviously be dictated by the texture, but generally never more than 3 inches).

Whizzing is done with the basic knife blade. If a recipe requires grated, shredded, or sliced ingredients, we specify which other disk or blade to use.

SLICING

There is nothing complicated about the way we slice ingredients. Our aim is to produce food with as much flavor and texture as possible and, as we have to achieve this in 10 minutes, both preparation and cooking are as speedy as possible. Since every minute counts, there is a danger that fastidious slicing may become counter-productive and take up too much time.

Often we find that precise slicing, measuring, and weighing are unnecessary and waste vital seconds – we prefer instead to go by appearance. For example, when cooking meat, fish fillets or boned poultry breasts very fast they will probably need to be sliced either in half lengthwise or into long thin strips.

A word of warning! Do not cut too finely: there is always the possibility that the pieces may collapse into an unappetizing pulp.

Vegetables can be sliced either with a knife or in the food processor. The method to use depends on quantity and personal preference. Frankly, unless large quantities are being prepared, it is often not worth dirtying the food processor.

SLIVERING & SHREDDING

Particularly for stir-frying, vegetables can also be slivered or shredded. To sliver, just cut them across at a sharp angle into pieces no wider than $\frac{1}{2}$ inch.

Shredding can be done with the hands or by thinly slicing bunched-up food: particularly lettuce, cabbage, or spinach leaves; and ham or boned chicken breasts.

SNIPPING

Perhaps we use our scissors more than most, but we think the quickest way to prepare herbs, bacon, ham, scallions, anchovy fillets – and sometimes even fish – is to snip them.

Snipping has many advantages: it is incredibly fast; it saves on dishwashing, as you can snip directly over – or into – a pan or dish; and it is labor-saving as it allows whole handfuls to be cut in one go.

ZESTING

As there is no time for marinating or slow simmers, we find that adding the zest of citrus fruit is a marvelous way of intensifying flavor and adding texture.

Of course zest should really be blanched (to tenderize and remove any bitterness), but we just do not have the time. For our purposes the best zest is the thinnest, with as little pith as possible. So when using a zester, try not to press it down too firmly against the fruit as this also brings up a thick layer of white and bitter pith.

PASTE-PAINTING

In 10-minute cuisine, paste-painting is the alternative to marinating. The secret to successful paste-painting lies in the paste – this must be strong-flavored, full-bodied, and thick-textured.

What the paste does while the food is cooking is to create a coating which seals in the flavor (both its own and that of the coated item) and adds to the taste and texture. The technique is fun and simple to use, and works best of all when grilling. Simply paint the paste evenly all over the food.

GRILLING AND BROILING

Everybody is familiar with grilling. All we want to add, when it comes to 10-minute cooking, is that the heat – whether applied from above or below – should be very hot and the food thinly sliced. (Particularly if you have an electric broiler, use any preparation time to get the broiler good and hot before you cook!)

SEARING

Searing, sometimes called "seizing," is very fast grilling or pan-frying in order to seal in juices and flavor. Seared food is often paste-painted first and the technique works particularly well with the firm strong flesh of red meat or salmon.

SAUTÉING OR PAN-FRYING

Again, this is a basic technique used by everybody. For our purposes, we first slice, snip, shred, or sliver the food into small pieces. Then, while sautéing, we keep the heat moderate to prevent the food from burning. This method means that you can finish the dish by making a quick sauce conveniently in the same pan.

STIR-FRYING

The Chinese are masters of this technique. It is an excellent way of cooking fresh food very fast and is ideal for 10-minute cooking. The food must be cut, sliced, or snipped into small pieces for successful stir-frying.

A wok – with its deep sides and rounded bottom – is essential. First oil or grease it lightly, then put it over a high heat. Once the food is added to the wok, use a wok scoop to keep it on the move – this also applies to Stir-fried Eggs (see page 50). The shape of the wok enables cooked food to be pushed up the sides while more ingredients are being put in the pan to be cooked. Obviously, always start with whatever takes longest to cook. Extra liquid is sometimes added for later simmering.

BLANCHING

This simply means plunging food – in our case, only vegetables – in boiling water for a minute or two to soften them slightly. They must then be refreshed quickly in cold water to stop the cooking and keep their color.

POACHING

Poaching is a gentle method of cooking which lends itself well to fish and poultry. Use a well-flavored poaching liquid – such as a good stock, wine or fruit juice – and bring it to a simmer. Keep it bubbling very gently over a low-to-moderate heat and bear in mind that the food is likely to toughen if the liquid is actually allowed to boil.

STEAM-BOILING

Much as we like conventional steaming, there is no time for it in 10-minute cuisine. The best alternative is steam-boiling. As you would expect, this method is a cross between boiling and steaming, using a minimum amount of liquid in a pan with a tight-fitting lid over a high heat. Steam-boiling is a very efficient way of cooking vegetables.

REDUCING

In conventional cooking, reduction is the slow process of boiling down a liquid to intensify its flavor and, very often, thicken its texture. In our terminology, all it means is that we turn up the heat a little and boil vigorously in an uncovered pan to generate maximum flavor in as short a time as possible.

FINISHING OR DEGLAZING

Finishing is an easy way of "deglazing" a pan to make a quick sauce. Once the food is cooked, remove it from the pan and keep it warm. Then add a little liquid, such as stock, wine, vinegar, cream – or even a pat of butter – to the cooking juices in the pan. Next turn up the heat and, using a wooden spoon, scrape and stir the sediment in the pan until the juices thicken to a sauce-like consistency. Then simply spoon this over the food.

WARMING PLATES

The way we cook does not allow for fancy presentation or trimmings, which is why we never individually plate food. Instead, we arrange it on a serving dish from which everyone may help themselves. We always try to warm the dish and, where appropriate, will try also to warm the plates. There are several quick ways of ensuring that the dishes and plates are warm:
1) Hold or place them under hot running water a minute or two and then let them drain.
2) Place them, one at a time, under a hot broiler for a second or two.
3) Where a safe fit allows, perch them on the tops of saucepans.

Soups

Soups are an integral part of our "10-minute" approach, whether served as an appetizer or as a main course.

Contrary to popular belief, there is no need to simmer a soup for hours – providing you start with fresh ingredients, full of flavor, which are then finely sliced, snipped, or zested.

We are not great fans of bouillon cubes – as we have yet to find one that does a better job than water and sea salt; however, stock is needed to cook some of these soups. Use either homemade (if you have the time and inclination) or buy fresh or frozen stock or canned broth.

As a guide to quantity we find that 5 cups of soup is about the right amount for 4 people.

Avocado, Spinach, and Lemon Soup (page 36)

NO-COOK SOUPS

Our "no-cook" cold soups really can be made in minutes and are breathtakingly simple – as long as you have a food processor!

To speed the process even further, we do not peel the vegetables – just give them a thorough wash and chop them roughly into pieces of a size the food processor can easily handle.

To keep no-cook soups as fresh-tasting as possible it is best to make them at the last minute. If you like them chilled, add a few ice cubes to the mixture while whizzing it in the processor, or float a couple in each serving bowl.

1 PINE NUT SOUP

Process a handful of pine nuts and a clove of garlic to a smooth paste. Add a couple of slices of whole wheat bread (crusts removed) and an egg, then process again. Slowly pour in $1\frac{1}{4}$ cups olive oil followed by $1\frac{1}{4}$ cups water and whizz to a smooth paste. Pour in 3 tablespoons of sherry vinegar and season to taste with sea salt and freshly ground black pepper. If the soup is too solid, add a little more water or some ice and whizz again.

2 AVOCADO, SPINACH, AND LEMON SOUP

Process 1 pound trimmed baby spinach leaves, then add a couple of roughly chopped ripe avocados and the juice of 1 lemon. Whizz until smooth, adding about 3 cups water or stock until the soup is the right consistency. Season to taste with Tabasco, sea salt, and freshly ground black pepper.

3 CUCUMBER AND TARRAGON SOUP

Peel, halve lengthwise, and scrape out the seeds of a hothouse cucumber. Process with a handful of fresh tarragon and $1\frac{1}{4}$ cups of plain yogurt. Season to taste with sea salt and freshly ground black pepper.

4 TOMATO SOUP

Roughly chop 1 pound ripe tomatoes. Whizz until fluffy and airy. Season to taste with sea salt, freshly ground black pepper, and a dash of sugar, if the tomatoes are not very sweet. Serve garnished with some fresh basil leaves.

5 MELON SOUP

Quarter 2 ripe cantaloupes, scrape out the seeds and scoop out the flesh. Process the flesh with 1 tablespoon honey, a handful of mint leaves, the juice of 1 lemon, and $\frac{2}{3}$ cup of plain sheep's milk yogurt. Season to taste with sea salt and freshly ground black pepper.

6 TARATOR

Peel, halve lengthwise, and scrape out the seeds of a hothouse cucumber. Process with a handful of walnuts, a couple of garlic cloves, some fresh parsley, 2 tablespoons of olive oil, and $1\frac{1}{4}$ cups of plain yogurt. If the soup is too solid, add ice cubes and whizz again. Season to taste.

HOT SOUPS

Edouard de Pomiane, the celebrated French gastronome of the 1930s and great master of the art of cooking in 10 minutes, had "an invariable rite." No matter what he was cooking, the first thing he did was to bring to a boil plenty of water.

For hot soups this certainly applies, although for some recipes it may be stock, or wine and water, which should be heated.

HERB VELOUTÉ

5 CUPS WATER
SMALL BUNCHES OF FRESH
  HERBS, INCLUDING: PARSLEY,
  WATERCRESS, CHERVIL, AND
  TARRAGON
½ CUP SOUR CREAM
SEA SALT AND FRESHLY GROUND
  BLACK PEPPER
BUTTER, TO FINISH

1 Bring the water to a boil.

2 Snip the herbs into a boiling water and simmer 5 minutes.

3 Process to a smooth texture. Whizz in the cream.

4 Season to taste and serve with a pat of butter on top of each plate of soup.

LETTUCE AND PEA SOUP

5 CUPS WATER
3 SLICES OF SMOKED BACON
2 SCALLIONS
½ POUND FROZEN PEAS
1 HEAD OF ROMAINE LETTUCE
FEW LEAVES OF SUMMER
  SAVORY (OR SPRIGS OF
  THYME)
⅔ CUP LIGHT CREAM
SEA SALT AND FRESHLY GROUND
  BLACK PEPPER

1 Bring the water to a boil in a kettle.

2 Heat a large saucepan, snip in the bacon and dry-fry 1 minute.

3 Snip in the scallions and cook until they are just softened.

4 Add the peas and the boiling water. Stir and simmer 2 minutes.

5 Snip in the lettuce and summer savory. Simmer a further 3 minutes.

6 Process to a smooth texture. Whizz in the cream and season to taste.

CARROT AND ORANGE SOUP

Use young baby carrots as they seldom need peeling, need hardly any cooking, and taste far fresher and sweeter than older woody varieties.

For extra depth of color, use a blood orange. Whatever you do, do not let the soup come to a boil as this will ruin the flavor.

1 POUND YOUNG CARROTS
5 CUPS WATER OR STOCK
2 TBSP BUTTER
3 SCALLIONS
1 TBSP GROUND CUMIN
1 ORANGE
½ CUP DRY VERMOUTH
SEA SALT AND FRESHLY GROUND
    BLACK PEPPER
SMALL BUNCH OF FRESH
    PARSLEY, TO FINISH

1 Bring the water to a boil in a teakettle.

2 Melt the butter in a large saucepan and snip the scallions into the butter. Add the cumin.

3 Rinse the carrots and finely shred them in the food processor, using the shredding blade. Add to the pan and soften a couple of minutes over a moderate heat.

4 Zest, then juice the orange. Stir the zest and vermouth into the carrot mixture.

5 Pour in the boiling water and simmer 5 minutes.

6 Add the orange juice and season to taste. Snip a little parsley over the soup to finish.

Clockwise from the top left: Carrot and Orange Soup; Lettuce and Pea Soup (page 37); Chinese soup (page 41)

CAULIFLOWER SOUP

This is a very filling soup which can be a meal in itself, served with Croûtons (see page 61) or buttered toast rubbed with garlic. Best results are obtained using a firm fresh cauliflower and a strong-flavored sharp Cheddar.

1 LARGE HEAD OF
  CAULIFLOWER
5 TBSP BUTTER
2½ CUPS CHICKEN STOCK
1¼ CUPS MILK
PINCH OF DRIED MARJORAM
¼ POUND SHARP CHEDDAR
NUTMEG
SEA SALT AND FRESHLY GROUND
  BLACK PEPPER

1 Roughly chop the cauliflower into florets and whizz to crumbs in the food processor.

2 Melt 4 tablespoons of the butter in a large saucepan and sauté the processed cauliflower over a moderate heat.

3 Add the chicken stock, milk, and dried marjoram. Bring to a boil, then reduce the heat and simmer a few minutes, stirring frequently.

4 Grate in the cheese along with nutmeg to taste and stir them in well.

5 Season to taste and finish by adding the remaining butter, cut into small pieces.

GARLIC SOUP

We have broken our 10-minute rule to include this recipe – even if the soup needs to simmer 15 minutes – as it requires virtually no preparation. It is adapted from *The Cuisine of Paul Bocuse* and when we first read and tried it, we could not believe that anything quite so basic could taste so complex – but it does!

7½ CUPS WATER
15 GARLIC CLOVES
2 CLOVES
3 FRESH SAGE LEAVES
2 TSP SEA SALT
1 FRENCH LOAF (BAGUETTE)
¼ POUND GRUYÈRE OR
  PARMESAN
OLIVE OIL
FRESHLY GROUND BLACK
  PEPPER

1 Heat the oven to 475°F.

2 Bring the water to a boil with the garlic, cloves, sage, salt, and pepper. Let simmer 15 minutes.

3 Meanwhile, slice the French bread and place it on a baking sheet.

4 Grate the cheese and scatter it over the bread along with a few drops of olive oil.

5 Bake in the oven until golden brown.

6 Place a couple of slices of the cooked bread in each soup plate, if necessary adjust the seasoning of the hot soup, and pour it into the plates.

CHINESE SOUP

For super-fast stir-frying, remember to shred or chop the ingredients very finely (see page 30). One short-cut you cannot take is to use a bouillon cube in this soup. A good stock, either homemade or purchased, is vital.

5 CUPS CHICKEN STOCK

2 GARLIC CLOVES

3 SCALLIONS

PIECE OF FRESH GINGERROOT, ABOUT 1 INCH

2 TBSP SUNFLOWER OIL

1 LARGE BONED CHICKEN BREAST HALF

¼ POUND OYSTER MUSHROOMS

1 HEAD OF NAPA CABBAGE (OR 1 ROMAINE LETTUCE)

¼ POUND BABY CORN

1 TBSP SOY SAUCE

¼ POUND BEANTHREAD NOODLES

SMALL BUNCH OF CILANTRO LEAVES

SEA SALT AND FRESHLY GROUND BLACK PEPPER

FEW DROPS OF SESAME OIL, TO FINISH

1 Bring the stock to a boil, reduce the heat and simmer gently.

2 In the food processor, whizz the garlic, scallions, and ginger to a paste.

3 Heat the oil in a wok until very hot, add the paste and stir-fry 1 minute.

4 Skin and shred the chicken, and stir-fry it in the wok 1 minute.

5 Roughly chop the oyster mushrooms, Napa cabbage, and corn. Add to the wok with the soy sauce and stir-fry another 1 minute.

6 Pour in the stock, break in the beanthread noodles, and stir.

7 Simmer a few minutes, and snip in the cilantro leaves.

8 Season to taste and sprinkle in a few drops of sesame oil to finish.

Pasta

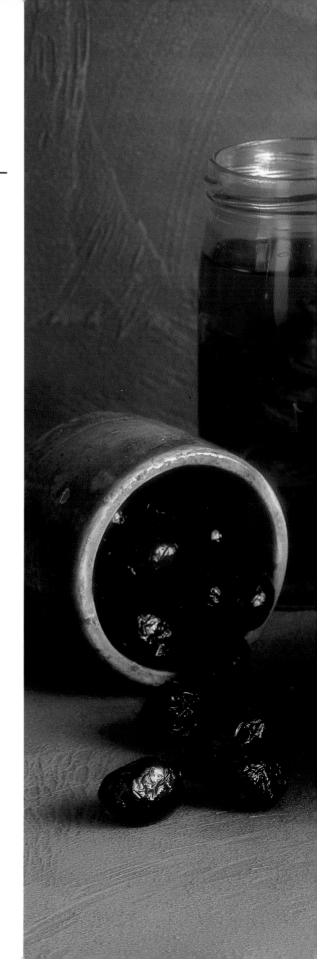

We would be quite lost without pasta – it is one of our staples. We eat it several times a week, and often serve it when we are entertaining friends.

The time-consuming part of pasta cooking is heating the large quantity of water required (you need about 5 cups water for each 4-ounce serving of pasta), but this can be greatly reduced if you boil the water in 2 pans.

Fresh pasta is currently enjoying great popularity and does cook very fast, but – unless it is made in front of our eyes – we are not convinced that it warrants the extra cost. We like the bite and taste of a good dried pasta, and we usually buy packages of one or other of the better known Italian brands made from hard durum wheat.

Depending on the shape you choose, the pasta may take a good 10 minutes to cook. We serve ours in the Italian manner "al dente" – just tender, but still with a bit of bite – which suits our very fast sauces.

Appetites and tastes vary, so we do not give exact quantities of pasta. However, a good guide is about 3-4 ounces per portion.

Tagliatelle with Sun-dried Tomato and Ripe Olive Sauce (page 44)

Our Cabinet and No-cook Sauces are robust and extremely simple to prepare. We have also included a few extra sauces in 12 Things to do with Cans (see page 20) or you may like to try dressing pasta with some of the sauces or compound butters from the Fish and Meat chapters (see pages 86 and 101).

KITCHEN CABINET SAUCES

Simply use the suggested preparations from page 18 as a sauce. You may, perhaps, add an extra ingredient (such as sliced mushrooms) or a herb or two (such as a couple of snipped leaves of fresh – or a small pinch of dried – basil, tarragon, or oregano). These sauces need no cooking: just return the cooked and drained pasta to the pan over a very low heat, pour in the sauce of your choice and stir well into the pasta. The heat from the pasta warms the sauce through.

1 LABNA CHEESE BALLS IN OIL

Pour some of the oil from the jar over the pasta. Mix it in well, season to taste with freshly ground black pepper, and then add a few whole or crushed labna balls.

2 SUN-DRIED TOMATO AND RIPE OLIVES

Snip 5 or 6 sun-dried tomatoes and a few pitted ripe olives. Pour some of the oil from the jar over the pasta, add the tomatoes and olives and mix well. Season to taste with sea salt and freshly ground black pepper.

3 CHILI OIL AND CILANTRO

Snip some fresh cilantro. Pour some chili oil (or a mixture of chili and olive oils) over the pasta, add the cilantro, and mix well. Season with sea salt.

4 ROASTED GARLIC AND PARSLEY

Snip some fresh parsley. Crush some cloves from a head of roasted garlic to extract the purée and add this to the parsley. Pour some good olive oil over the pasta, add the garlic and parsley, and mix well. Season with freshly ground black pepper.

NO-COOK SAUCES

Nothing could be easier to make — or fresher tasting — than a no-cook sauce. You mix it into the cooked and drained pasta in exactly the same way as you would a cabinet sauce. The residual heat is enough to warm it through and lightly cook it, should that be necessary.

1 CRÈME FRAÎCHE WITH DILL AND SALMON CAVIAR

Snip a handful of fresh dill over 1¼ cups of crème fraîche. Season with freshly ground black pepper and stir well. Mix into the cooked and drained pasta. Top each serving with a spoonful of salmon caviar.

2 BLUE CHEESE, CREAM, AND ARUGULA

In the food processor, whizz 3 ounces blue cheese, a handful of arugula leaves (reserving a few whole ones) and ⅔ cup of light cream to a thickish sauce. Mix into the cooked and drained pasta, snip over the remaining arugula leaves. Season with freshly ground black pepper.

3 FRESH TOMATO AND MINT

In the food processor, roughly whizz about 1 pound ripe fresh tomatoes, 1 scallion, 1 garlic clove, and a handful of mint leaves. Stir in a little olive oil. Season with sea salt, freshly ground black pepper, and a pinch of sugar, if the tomatoes aren't sweet enough. Mix into the cooked and drained pasta.

4 RAW EGG, PARMA HAM, AND CHIVES

Beat a couple of eggs with a minced garlic clove and ⅔ cup of light cream. Snip some Parma ham and chives into the mixture. Stir into the cooked and drained pasta. Season with freshly ground black pepper.

5 ANCHOVY, CAPERS, PARSLEY, AND THYME

Snip 3 or 4 anchovy fillets with 1 tablespoon each of fresh parsley and thyme. Add some drained capers and olive oil. Stir into the cooked and drained pasta. Season with freshly ground black pepper.

6 WALNUT AND THYME

In the food processor, whizz a handful of walnuts to a smooth paste. Add a few sprigs of fresh thyme, a couple of eggs, some lemon zest, and sea salt and freshly ground black pepper to taste and whizz again to blend. Add 1 or 2 tablespoons of olive oil and stir into the cooked and drained pasta.

7 SPINACH, CREAM CHEESE, AND PARMESAN

In the food processor, whizz 5 ounces cream cheese and 2 ounces Parmesan until smooth. Add about $\frac{1}{2}$ pound baby spinach leaves and $\frac{2}{3}$ cup of light cream and whizz again briefly. Stir into the cooked and drained pasta.

8 SHREDDED ZUCCHINI WITH PINE NUTS AND TARRAGON

Shred 1 or 2 zucchini in the food processor, using the shredding blade. Snip over a few tarragon leaves and add a handful of pine nuts and 1 or 2 tablespoons of olive oil. Season with sea salt and freshly ground black pepper. Mix into the cooked and drained pasta.

Left: Shredded Zucchini with Pine Nuts and Tarragon over fusilli; Right: Crème Fraîche with Dill and Salmon Caviar (page 45) over plain tagliatelle.

Eggs

Egg dishes are a useful standby in 10-minute cuisine as practically everyone has at least half a dozen eggs in the refrigerator.

We have already mentioned in the introductory section on ingredients that we only buy eggs from trusted suppliers who can guarantee them to be totally safe. It is also a good idea to check each egg by first breaking it into a separate container.

All the following recipes are for four extra large eggs. Allow 1 per person for a half-plate portion and 2 for a full plate.

*Parsley, Chive, and Tarragon Eggs
(page 50)*

STIR-FRIED EGGS

These are a sort of cross between scrambled eggs and an omelette, although stir-fried eggs are cooked at a higher temperature in a wok. It helps the process if the eggs are at room temperature before being cooked, and the oil (ideally sunflower, grapeseed, or light olive) should be well heated before adding the eggs.

First beat the eggs with a little extra liquid (water, or chicken or vegetable stock) then pour this mixture into the heated oil in the wok. Using a scoop or chopsticks, keep the eggs on the move. The result is delicately-flavored golden strips of lightly cooked eggs.

BASIC STIR-FRIED EGGS

Heat 1 tablespoon of oil in a wok until hot, swirling it around. Lightly beat 4 eggs with 2 tablespoons water, or chicken or vegetable stock. Season to taste with sea salt and freshly ground black pepper. Pour into the wok and stir-fry until the eggs are just cooked and golden in color.

1 MUSHROOM, SCALLION, AND CORIANDER EGGS

Heat 1 tablespoon of oil in a wok and swirl it around. Add a pinch of crushed coriander seeds and a handful of finely chopped mushrooms. Snip in 1-2 scallions and stir-fry a minute or two. Lightly beat 4 eggs with 2 tablespoons of water or stock, season, and pour into the wok. Stir-fry until the eggs are cooked.

2 PARSLEY, CHIVE, AND TARRAGON EGGS

Heat 2 tablespoons of oil with a pat of butter in a wok and swirl it around. Lightly beat 4 eggs with 2 tablespoons of water or stock, season, snip in a handful of the herbs, and pour into the wok. Stir-fry until the eggs are cooked.

3 SHRIMP, GINGER, AND SHERRY EGGS

Heat 1 tablespoon of oil in a wok and swirl it around. Add a minced garlic clove and a finely chopped piece of gingerroot (about 1 inch) and stir-fry a minute or two. Tip in a handful of peeled cooked shrimp and stir-fry 1 minute. Lightly beat 4 eggs with 1 tablespoon each of water and sherry, add a dash of soy sauce, season, and pour into the wok. Stir-fry until the eggs are cooked.

4 OLIVE, SUN-DRIED TOMATO, AND HERB EGGS

Heat 1 tablespoon of olive oil in a wok and swirl it around. Lightly beat 4 eggs with 2 tablespoons of water or stock and season. Add a few pitted and chopped ripe olives, and snip in a couple of sun-dried tomatoes and a few sprigs each of fresh marjoram and oregano. Pour into the wok and stir-fry until the eggs are cooked.

5 SMOKED TROUT AND DILL EGGS

Heat 2 tablespoons of oil with a pat of butter in a wok and swirl it around. Lightly beat 4 eggs with 2 tablespoons of water or stock. Season, add a few slivers of smoked trout, and snip in some dill. Pour into the wok and stir-fry until the eggs are cooked. Then beat in 1 or 2 tablespoons of sour cream.

6 HAM AND LEEK EGGS

Heat 1 tablespoon of oil in a wok and swirl it around. Add the finely chopped white of 1 leek and stir-fry 1 minute. Lightly beat 4 eggs with 2 tablespoons water or stock and 1 teaspoon of Dijon mustard and season. Snip in a slice of cooked ham, pour into the wok, and stir-fry until the eggs are cooked.

EGGAHS

They are a sort of cross between a quiche filling and an omelette. Our eggahs are cooked in a heavy-based omelette pan and then finished under the broiler.

In order for them to be crisp on the outside while still moist and barely set inside, eggahs must be about 2 inches thick. For our 4-egg eggah we use a 7-inch pan.

Either stir the filling into the mixture and cook it like a thick omelette or sauté the filling separately in the pan, pour the eggs on top, and then lift the filling to allow the eggs to set underneath.

BASIC EGGAH

In a heavy-based omelette pan, heat 1 tablespoon of oil with a pat of butter. Stir in any cooked and chopped suitable leftovers (chicken, potatoes, peas, salmon, etc) and sauté 1 minute. Beat 4 eggs with a tablespoon of milk, season with sea salt and freshly ground black pepper, and pour over the filling, lifting it to allow the mixture to run underneath. Cook until just set, then sprinkle with a little extra oil or dot with butter and brown under a hot broiler.

1 TWO-CHEESE EGGAH

In a heavy-based omelette pan, heat 2 teaspoons of oil with a pat of butter. Beat 4 eggs with 1 tablespoon of milk. Stir in a handful each of Mozzarella and Parmesan cheeses, cut into slivers, and season. Pour into the pan and cook until set. Sprinkle with extra cheese and brown under the broiler.

2 BLUE CHEESE AND SCALLION EGGAH

In a heavy-based omelette pan, heat 2 teaspoons of oil with a pat of butter. Beat 4 eggs with 1 tablespoon of milk. Crumble in 2 ounces blue cheese. Snip in 1 scallion and season. Pour into the pan and cook until set. Sprinkle with extra cheese and brown under the broiler.

3 ZUCCHINI, TOMATO, AND THYME EGGAH

In a heavy-based omelette pan, heat 1 tablespoon of olive oil with a pat of butter. Stir in 2 tablespoons each of chopped zucchini and tomatoes, snip in a few sprigs of fresh thyme, and cook a couple of minutes to soften. Beat 4 eggs with 1 tablespoon of milk. Season, pour into the pan, and cook until set. Sprinkle with olive oil and brown under the broiler.

4 OYSTER MUSHROOM EGGAH

In a heavy-based omelette pan, heat 1 tablespoon of olive oil with a pat of butter. Stir in a handful of sliced oyster mushrooms with a minced $\frac{1}{2}$ garlic clove and sauté 1 or 2 minutes. Beat 4 eggs with 1 tablespoon of milk. Season, pour into the pan, and cook until set. Dot with butter and brown under the broiler.

5 ASPARAGUS TIP AND CREAM CHEESE EGGAH

In a heavy-based omelette pan, heat 2 teaspoons of oil with a pat of butter. Stir in a handful of asparagus tips and sauté a couple of minutes. Beat 4 eggs with 1 tablespoon each of milk and cream cheese. Season, pour into the pan, and cook until set. Dot with cream cheese and brown.

6 SPINACH AND PARMESAN EGGAH

In a heavy-based omelette pan, heat 2 teaspoons of oil with a pat of butter. Snip in a handful of washed and well-drained spinach and sweat 1 minute. Beat 4 eggs with 1 tablespoon each of milk and light cream. Grate in a small piece of Parmesan and a little nutmeg. Season, pour into the pan, and cook until set. Sprinkle with more Parmesan and brown.

EGGS EN COCOTTE

For this classic dish, in which eggs are baked in buttered ramekins set in a bain marie in the oven, use a baking pan half-filled with water which has been boiled in a teakettle to speed up the process.

One egg en cocotte is a half-plate portion, and 2 a full plate. As well as the recipes below, try eggs en cocotte with Hollandaise Sauce (see page 84) or our compound butters (see pages 86-7 and 101).

BASIC EGGS EN COCOTTE

Heat the oven to 350°F and boil a teakettle of water. Divide 3 tablespoons butter into 4 pieces and spread each into one of 4 small ramekins, ensuring that the sides and bottoms are all well greased.

Snip a few chopped chives into each ramekin and then trickle 2 teaspoons of light cream into each. Break an egg into each ramekin and trickle a little more cream over that. Season lightly and put the ramekins in a baking pan.

Pour boiling water from the teakettle into the baking pan to come halfway up the sides of the ramekins. Bake 7-10 minutes – the exact timing depends on how you like your eggs to be cooked.

Watercress, Herb, and Cream Cheese Eggs

1 MUSHROOM, SHALLOT, AND CREAM EGGS

Finely chop about 2 ounces mushrooms and 1 shallot. Put equal portions of this mixture into each ramekin. Trickle over a little light cream and season. Break an egg into each ramekin and then trickle over a little extra cream. Bake as above.

2 CREAM AND CHEESE EGGS

Into each ramekin, put about 1 tablespoon of shredded Gruyère. Trickle over a little heavy cream, add a drop or two of Kirsch, and season. Break 1 egg into each ramekin and trickle over a little extra cream and a sprinkling of shredded cheese. Bake as above.

3 RICOTTA, CHILI AND CUMIN EGGS

Beat 4 ounces ricotta with a small pinch each of ground cumin, turmeric, and chili powder. Into each ramekin spread some of the mixture. Break 1 egg into each ramekin and dot with a little butter. Bake as above.

4 SMOKED HADDOCK AND CREAM EGGS

Into each ramekin, place some small pieces of smoked haddock (finnan haddie). Trickle over a little light cream and season with cayenne. Break 1 egg into each ramekin and trickle over a little extra cream. Bake as above.

5 SPINACH AND ANCHOVY EGGS

Into each ramekin, put some finely chopped spinach, capers, and anchovy fillet. Trickle over a little light cream and season with freshly ground black pepper. Break 1 egg into each ramekin and dot with a little butter. Bake as above.

6 WATERCRESS, HERB, AND CREAM CHEESE EGGS

Into each ramekin, put some finely chopped watercress, parsley, savory, and lemon balm. Spoon in a little cream cheese and season. Break 1 egg into each ramekin and dot with extra cream cheese. Bake as above.

Salads

For us, there is no such thing as a meal without a salad: as an appetizer, a main course, or a side dish. We eat at least one salad every day, and soon suffer serious withdrawal symptoms if we have to go without.

Luckily, the range of salad leaves generally available in this country has improved enormously in the last few years and now most major supermarket chains stock a reasonably good selection.

The following leaves and herbs are all widely available and a good bet in season: romaine, bibb, Boston, leaf, red leaf, and iceberg lettuce; chicories including curly endive (or frisée), Belgian endive, and radicchio; field lettuce (also known as corn salad lamb's tongue or mâche), arugula, watercress, baby spinach, sorrel, dandelion greens and purslane.

Most supermarkets also now sell growing herbs in plastic containers, which can be kept on the windowsill. Fresh parsley, chives, and cilantro we sometimes snip into dressings; chives, thyme, basil, chervil, cilantro, sage, tarragon, summer and winter savory, borage, hyssop, parsley, mint, marjoram, and oregano we snip over the leaves.

Flowers or seed tops, such as hyssop, nasturtium, chives, arugula, radish pods and spinach heads, can also be used whole or snipped into salads.

Whatever the mix, remember to wash and spin-dry everything thoroughly (see page 25), as soggy leaves water down the dressing. Tearing and trimming leaves with the hands is better and easier.

Sealed plastic bags of ready trimmed and washed mixed salad leaves are also now readily available. These are expensive, with a short shelf life (do check for any discoloration before buying!), but they can save precious time.

When making up a salad, bear in mind the color, taste, and texture balance, and use a good variety of different types of leaves for an interesting combination.

For extra crunch, sprinkle the leaves with sea salt.

You may have noticed that some old standbys, such as tomatoes, cucumber, carrots, white and red cabbage, sweet red and green peppers, radishes, and beet are missing from our list. We have not included them because we don't feel that they belong in a mixed-leaf salad.

DOLLOP DRESSINGS

These are a cross between a salad dressing and a dip, and are best spooned on the side of the plate rather than tossed into a salad. Alternatively, heap the dollop of dressing on a pile of leaves – but make no attempt at coating! We particularly like these dressings with grated vegetables and crudité sticks and florets.

1 MAYONNAISE

In a food processor, whizz 2 egg yolks with 1 tablespoon of lemon juice and 1 teaspoon of Dijon mustard. With the food processor running, trickle in 1¼ cups mixed olive and sunflower oils and process until thick and creamy. Add 1 teaspoon of lemon juice or water, whizz again, and season with sea salt and freshly ground black pepper.

2 CREAM MAYONNAISE

As Mayonnaise above, but at the end add 2 tablespoons of light cream instead of the extra 1 teaspoon of lemon juice or water.

3 HERB MAYONNAISE

As Mayonnaise above, but add a handful of herbs, such as parsley, chives, tarragon, and marjoram, with the lemon juice or water.

4 BLUE CHEESE DRESSING

Whizz a generous piece (about 3 ounces) of blue cheese with 3 tablespoons of sour cream, 2 tablespoons of olive oil, 1 teaspoon of lemon juice, and freshly ground black pepper until smooth.

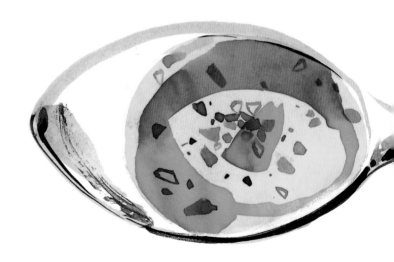

COATING DRESSINGS

The most important thing for any dressing, especially one which is to coat all the leaves, is the quality of the ingredients – only the best oils, such as extra-virgin olive oil, will do. This is not as extravagant as it sounds since you do not need much.

One essential point is always to use a big enough salad bowl to be able to toss the salad comfortably. First mix your dressing in a small bowl or jar until well blended and then either pour it into the empty salad bowl, adding the leaves on top, or pour it over the salad in the bowl. Either way, toss it in the bowl until all the leaves are well coated.

(We tend to use our hands to dress the salads, which is very easy and efficient.) We also like our salads just lightly coated, so we have no hard and fast rules about quantities. In this chapter, however – as elsewhere in the book – all our recipes are for 4 people.

How much dressing is needed depends entirely on how lightly or generously coated you like your salad to be. A good guideline, however, is 6 tablespoons of dressing for each 12 ounces salad leaves. Go easy on the vinegar: no more than 2 tablespoons of those 6 should be vinegar! Our favorite ratio is 5:1 oil to vinegar. Sea salt we use more liberally in salad dressings than in any other type of dish: one trick is to go on adding salt to the dressing, in small amounts, until it stops tasting oily.

1 POUR-OVER DRESSING

Trickle a good oil (see above) over a salad and toss. Add a pinch of sea salt, freshly ground black pepper, and, if you like, a squirt of fresh lemon juice. Toss again.

2 VINAIGRETTE

In a cup, mix together 5 tablespoons of olive oil with 1 tablespoon of white wine vinegar, 1 teaspoon of Dijon mustard, and sea salt and freshly ground black pepper to taste.

3 GARLIC VINAIGRETTE

As for Vinaigrette, but add 1 small minced garlic clove.

4 HERB VINAIGRETTE

As for Vinaigrette, but add a handful of snipped chives or tarragon leaves.

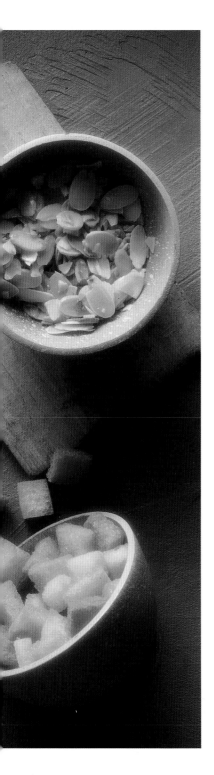

5 EGG VINAIGRETTE

In a cup, beat together 1 egg yolk with 1 teaspoon of Dijon mustard and 1 teaspoon of lemon juice. Slowly trickle in 6 tablespoons of olive oil, beating continuously. Season.

6 CREAM VINAIGRETTE

In a cup, combine 1 tablespoon of light cream with 2 teaspoons of sherry vinegar. Beat in 5 tablespoons of olive oil and season.

7 ANCHOVY VINAIGRETTE

Snip a couple of drained anchovy fillets into a small bowl and add 1 small minced garlic clove. Beat in 5 tablespoons of olive oil, 2 teaspoons of lemon juice, and season.

8 TAHINI DRESSING

In a cup, beat 2 tablespoons of tahini with 5 tablespoons of plain yogurt, the juice of $\frac{1}{2}$ a lemon, $\frac{1}{2}$ a minced garlic clove, a pinch of ground cumin, and sea salt and freshly ground black pepper.

Herb Hamburger (page 100); served with Mushroom Butter (page 101) and a green salad dressed with Egg Vinaigrette, Croūtons, and Sliced Almonds (page 61)

9 ORIENTAL DRESSING

In a cup, beat 3 tablespoons of soy sauce with 3 tablespoons of water, 2 teaspoons of sesame oil, and 1 teaspoon of ground ginger.

10 SOY SAUCE DRESSING

Snip a handful of fresh cilantro leaves into a cup. Mix in 2 tablespoons of soy sauce, 2 tablespoons of water, 1 tablespoon of sunflower oil, 1 teaspoon of sherry vinegar, 2 teaspoons of Dijon mustard, and a pinch of sugar.

11 TOMATO AND CHILI DRESSING

In the food processor, whizz a ripe tomato with 1 tablespoon of wine vinegar, 2 tablespoons of chili oil, a pinch of sugar, and season to taste with sea salt and freshly ground black pepper.

12 CILANTRO AND PARSLEY DRESSING

Snip $\frac{1}{2}$ a scallion and a handful each of cilantro and parsley leaves into a bowl. Mix in the juice of $\frac{1}{2}$ a lemon, 3 tablespoons of olive oil, and 3 tablespoons of light cream, and season to taste with sea salt and freshly ground black pepper.

BITS & PIECES FOR SALADS

Scatter these on top of a mixed, dressed, and tossed salad to add extra crunch and flavor and to improve appearance.

For interesting salads, experiment with combinations of more than one item at a time, such as Croûtons, Parmesan, and Ripe Olives.

Remember, however, that some of these toppings may be very salty, so cut down on the sea salt accordingly when seasoning the salad.

1 AVOCADO

Peel, pit, and chop a ripe avocado and sprinkle the flesh liberally with lemon juice. Good with spinach, endive and other bitter leaves, and works well with Croûtons and Anchovy Vinaigrette.

2 SNOW PEAS

Blanch a handful of trimmed snow peas 1 or 2 minutes. Drain, refresh in cold water, and dry. These add an interesting contrast of texture to most salads and are especially good with Baby Corn and Tahini Dressing.

3 BROCCOLI

Trim a head or two of broccoli into tiny florets. Blanch 1 or 2 minutes. Drain, refresh in cold water, and dry. Good with Ripe Olives and Tomato and Chili Dressing, or a strongly flavored oil such as walnut or sesame.

4 BABY CORN

Chop a handful of baby corn. Blanch 1 or 2 minutes. Drain, refresh in cold water, and dry. These add texture and a touch of sweetness and are especially good with Oriental Dressing.

5 STRAWBERRIES

Halve or quarter some ripe strawberries and sprinkle with black pepper. These look particularly pretty on top of an early summer leaf salad and are especially refreshing with chopped mint and Vinaigrette.

6 ORANGE

Peel and thinly slice a couple of oranges. Good with Belgian endive, tarragon, Walnuts, and Cream Vinaigrette.

7 RIPE OLIVES

Pit and chop a handful of ripe olives and toss into a dressed salad. Good with fennel or lettuce and Garlic Vinaigrette.

8 PARMESAN

Sprinkle some grated Parmesan over a dressed leaf salad. Good with mixed lettuces and Anchovy Vinaigrette.

9 LABNA BALLS

Crumble a few labna balls over the salad, using the oil from the jar as a dressing (see page 18). Good with Belgian endive, arugula, and other winter leaves.

10 BLUE CHEESE

Break a piece of blue cheese into small pieces and sprinkle over a dressed leaf salad. Especially good with spinach or dandelion greens and Vinaigrette.

11 WALNUTS

Chop a handful of walnuts. These add a interesting richness to winter leaves and watercress and are especially good with Cream Vinaigrette.

12 SLICED ALMONDS

Heat a little oil in a skillet. Add a handful of flaked almonds and sauté them until golden brown. Drain on paper towels and sprinkle with sea salt. Good with sweet summer leaves and Egg Vinaigrette.

13 PINE NUTS

Heat a little oil in a skillet. Add a handful of pine nuts and sauté them 1 or 2 minutes. Drain on paper towels. Good with a herby salad and Garlic Vinaigrette.

14 HAZELNUTS

Broil a handful of hazelnuts for a few minutes, shaking the pan a couple of times so they brown evenly. Sprinkle with sea salt. Good with lettuce and chicory (curly endive). These are among the best and simplest salad dressings.

15 PISTACHIOS

Broil a handful of shelled pistachios for a couple of minutes to heat them through. Sprinkle with sea salt. Good with Cream Vinaigrette.

16 POPPY SEEDS

Sprinkle a generous handful of poppy seeds over a dressed salad. Good with scallions and Egg Vinaigrette.

17 SESAME SEEDS

Toast a handful of sesame seeds in a dry skillet 1 or 2 minutes and sprinkle over a dressed salad. Good with Oriental Dressing.

18 SUNFLOWER SEEDS

Toast a handful of sunflower seeds in a dry skillet for 2 or 3 minutes. Sprinkle with sea salt and toss into a dressed salad. Good with a mild sweetish salad and Cream Vinaigrette.

19 DILL AND FENNEL SEEDS

Mix a pinch each of dill and fennel seeds with some sea salt and a drop or 2 of lemon juice. Toss into a dressed salad. Good with bitter leaves and Vinaigrette.

20 CROUTONS

Cut off the crusts from a couple of slices of bread, then cut the bread into small squares. Rub the inside of a skillet with a clove of garlic, heat a little olive oil and a pat of butter in it, and fry the bread until evenly crisp and golden. Drain on paper towels. A good all-rounder, adding great texture and pungency.

APPETIZER & MAIN COURSE SALADS

Normally most of our dishes work just as well as main courses as they do as appetizers. However, in the case of salads, some – such as Melon, Carrot and Lime Juice, Zucchini and Basil, and Leek – are meant only as appetizers and will not do as main courses.

MELON SALAD

◐

Use whichever variety of melon is in season, the riper the better.

½ SMALL ONION
1 TBSP SUGAR
1 TSP MUSTARD POWDER
2 TBSP WHITE WINE VINEGAR
4 TBSP SUNFLOWER OIL
1 CANTALOUPE OR OTHER
  MELON
1 ORANGE
1 LARGE PEAR
½ POUND CHICORY (CURLY
  ENDIVE) LEAVES
1 TBSP POPPY SEEDS

1   Whizz the onion, sugar, mustard powder, white wine vinegar, and oil until smooth.

2   Pour the dressing into a bowl and chill in the freezer while preparing the salad.

3   Quarter the melon and remove the seeds. Run a knife between the skin and flesh to separate the flesh and then cut it into slices.

4   Peel the orange and separate into segments.

5   Peel and quarter the pear. Remove the core and cut the flesh into slices.

6   Arrange the chicory leaves in a large salad bowl.

7   Scatter the prepared fruits over the top.

8   Sprinkle the chilled dressing over the salad followed by the poppy seeds.

CHICKEN LIVER AND CHILI SALAD

●

½ POUND CHICKEN LIVERS
3 TBSP CHILI OIL AND ½ CHILI IN
  OIL (SEE PAGE 19)
1 GARLIC CLOVE
1 SCALLION
SMALL HANDFUL OF CILANTRO
  LEAVES
¾ POUND MIXED SALAD LEAVES
2 TBSP OLIVE OIL
2 TBSP BUTTER
2 TBSP WHITE WINE VINEGAR
SEA SALT AND FRESHLY GROUND
  BLACK PEPPER

1   Trim and slice the chicken livers. Rinse and pat them dry with paper towels.

2   In a sauté pan, heat the chili oil.

3   Finely chop the garlic clove and 1 chili from the oil. Add these to the pan.

4   Snip in the scallions and the cilantro. Add the chicken livers, stir, and sauté the mixture over a moderate heat a few minutes, depending on how pink the livers are to be.

5   Meanwhile, wash and spin-dry the salad leaves. Tip them into a salad bowl and sprinkle them with olive oil and sea salt.

6   Using a slotted spoon, remove the chicken livers from the pan and add them to the leaves.

7 Add the butter to the pan and swirl until melted. Pour in the vinegar and turn up the heat. Using a wooden spoon, scrape the sediment in the pan to deglaze it until most of the vinegar has been boiled off.

8 Pour the deglazed pan juices over the salad and season.

Chicken Liver and Chili Salad

CARROT AND LIME JUICE SALAD

◑

To save time use small sweet young carrots, as they do not require peeling.

¾ POUND YOUNG CARROTS
3 SCALLIONS
PIECE OF FRESH GINGERROOT, ABOUT 1 INCH ACROSS
6 TBSP CHILI OIL
JUICE OF ½ LIME
SEA SALT

1   Rinse the carrots and shred in the food processor, using the shredding blade. Tip into a salad bowl.

2   Snip the scallions over a small bowl. Grate in the ginger, add the oil and lime juice. Season with salt and whisk together.

3   Pour the dressing over the salad and toss.

ZUCCHINI AND BASIL SALAD

◑

Again, use young vegetables – not only do large zucchini need peeling, but they are inclined to have a poor watery texture and a slightly bitter taste.

¾ POUND BABY ZUCCHINI
1 GARLIC CLOVE
½ CUP OLIVE OIL
1 LEMON
HANDFUL OF BASIL LEAVES
SEA SALT AND FRESHLY GROUND BLACK PEPPER

1   Rinse the zucchini and shred with the garlic in the food processor, using the shredding blade.

2   Warm 6 tablespoons of the oil in a sauté pan and tip in the zucchini.

3   Squeeze the juice from the lemon and add this juice to the pan. Stir a couple of minutes and season with salt and pepper.

4   Tip into a salad bowl and sprinkle in a little extra oil. Snip over the basil leaves and toss.

LEEK SALAD

◑

1 POUND LEEKS
2 EGGS
2 SCALLIONS
SMALL BUNCH OF FLAT-LEAF PARSLEY
1 TBSP CAPERS
6 TBSP OLIVE OIL
2 TBSP RED WINE VINEGAR
SEA SALT AND FRESHLY GROUND BLACK PEPPER

1   Bring 2 saucepans of water to a boil.

2   Meanwhile, rinse and trim the leeks and then slice them.

3   Add the eggs to 1 saucepan of water and boil 6 minutes.

4   Add the leeks to the other pan of water and simmer 1-2 minutes.

5   Drain the leeks and pat dry.

6   Snip the scallions and parsley into a small bowl and add the capers.

7   Shell the eggs under cold running water, snip them into the bowl, and mix together with a fork.

8   Add the oil and vinegar to the bowl, season, and beat the dressing together well.

9   Arrange the leeks on a plate and pour over the dressing.

Leek Salad

TWO-CHEESE SALAD

●

There is no need to buy expensive imported goats' cheese for this salad, as it is combined with Mozzarella. Choose one of the many factory-made "logs," carefully remove the rind (which can have an unpleasant taste), and cut the cheese into small slices or slivers.

Make the most of the interesting range of flavored breads now to be found in many supermarkets, and specialty bakeries and grocers: such as onion, walnut, raisin, olive, or garlic.

4 SLICES BREAD, PREFERABLY
 FLAVORED (SEE ABOVE)
¼ POUND MOZZARELLA
¼ POUND GOATS' CHEESE
¾ POUND MIXED SALAD LEAVES
2 TBSP WALNUT OIL
SEA SALT AND FRESHLY GROUND
 BLACK PEPPER

1 Heat the broiler and toast the bread on one side.

2 Meanwhile, cut the cheeses into slices, removing any rind.

3 Put a slice of Mozzarella on the untoasted side of each piece of bread. Cover with a slice of goats' cheese, season with pepper, and return to the broiler until the cheese has melted and is golden brown.

4 Meanwhile, wash and spin-dry the salad leaves. Tip them out on a plate or into a salad bowl, sprinkle with oil and sea salt, and toss.

5 Add the toasted cheese slices to the leaves.

CHICKEN AND SUN-DRIED TOMATO SALAD

●

2 CUPS WATER
¾ CUP DRY WHITE WINE
1 CELERY STALK
1 BAY LEAF
4 BLACK PEPPERCORNS
3 BONED CHICKEN BREAST
 HALVES
¾ POUND MIXED SALAD LEAVES
4 SUN-DRIED TOMATOES IN OIL
 (SEE PAGE 18)
4 LABNA BALLS IN OIL (SEE
 PAGE 18)
SEA SALT AND FRESHLY GROUND
 BLACK PEPPER

1   In a sauté pan, bring to a boil the water and wine, along with celery, bay leaf, and peppercorns. Reduce the heat immediately and leave to simmer.

2   Meanwhile, skin the chicken breast pieces and cut them in half lengthwise.

3   Add the chicken to the pan and simmer 6 minutes, or until cooked through.

4   Meanwhile, wash and spin-dry the salad leaves, then tip them into a salad bowl.

5   Snip the sun-dried tomatoes over the leaves and spoon a little of their oil over as well.

6   Crumble the labna balls over the salad and spoon a little of their oil over the salad.

7   Drain the cooked chicken breasts, cut them into strips, and add to the salad.

8   Season and toss well together.

EGG AND BLUE CHEESE SALAD

●

Any leaves work well in this recipe, but it is particularly good with field lettuce and chicory (curly endive).

If you cannot find Roquefort, buy any strong-flavored creamy blue cheese.

¾ POUND MIXED SALAD LEAVES
2 TBSP BUTTER
4 SLICES SMOKED BACON
3 OUNCES ROQUEFORT OR
    OTHER BLUE CHEESE
FEW SPRIGS OF FRESH THYME
4 TBSP WHITE WINE
4 TBSP LIGHT CREAM
DASH OF VINEGAR
4 EGGS
FRESHLY GROUND BLACK
    PEPPER

1   Bring a large saucepan of water to a boil.

2   Wash and spin-dry the salad leaves and tip them into a salad bowl.

3   Melt the butter in a sauté pan. Snip in the bacon and sauté a couple of minutes over a moderate heat.

4   Crumble in the cheese and stir until it starts to melt.

5   Snip in the thyme and add the white wine and cream. Stir occasionally until smooth, and then season with pepper.

6   Add the vinegar to a boiling water and reduce the heat to a simmer. Stir the water, crack the eggs into the water one at a time, and poach them 2 or 3 minutes, until the whites are just set.

7   Using a slotted spoon, carefully lift out the poached eggs, drain and put them on top of the salad leaves.

8   Pour over the cheese and bacon dressing.

MUSHROOM SALAD

◖

This salad tastes best if a number of different types of mushroom are used: particularly brown caps and oyster mushrooms and – if the budget runs to it – fresh wild mushrooms, such as chanterelles and cèpes.

1 POUND MIXED MUSHROOMS
   (SEE ABOVE)
1 GARLIC CLOVE
3 TBSP OLIVE OIL
2 TBSP BUTTER
1 LEMON
SEA SALT AND FRESHLY GROUND
   BLACK PEPPER
SMALL BUNCH OF FRESH
   CHIVES

1   Wipe the mushrooms and slice them if they are large.

2   Rub a sauté pan with the garlic. Heat the oil and sauté the mushrooms over a moderate heat 2 or 3 minutes, stirring frequently.

3   Cut the butter into small pieces and dot it over the mushrooms. Stir until the butter has melted.

4   Tip the cooked mushrooms out on a suitable dish.

5   Squeeze the juice from the lemon and sprinkle it over the mushrooms.

6   Season with sea salt and pepper. Snip over the chives.

BACON AND CRUMB SALAD

●

Spinach and arugula are our favorite leaves for this salad.

For a nutty taste and texture, make crumbs from day-old whole wheat bread.

4 TBSP OLIVE OIL
4 SLICES BACON
¾ POUND MIXED SALAD LEAVES
1 RIPE AVOCADO
JUICE OF ½ LEMON
2 THICK SLICES OF DAY-OLD
    BREAD
SMALL BUNCH OF PARSLEY
FEW SPRIGS OF THYME AND
    MARJORAM
1 GARLIC CLOVE
2 TBSP WHITE WINE VINEGAR
SEA SALT AND FRESHLY GROUND
    BLACK PEPPER

1   Heat half the oil in a medium-sized skillet. Snip in the bacon and sauté over a moderate heat until cooked.

2   Meanwhile, wash and spin-dry the salad leaves and tip them into a large bowl.

3   Halve, pit, peel, and chop the avocado. Add to the bowl and sprinkle with lemon juice and sea salt.

4   Using a slotted spoon, remove the bacon from the pan and add to the salad.

5   In the food processor, whizz the bread with the herbs and garlic to make coarse crumbs.

6   Heat the remaining oil in the pan. Add the prepared crumbs to the pan and stir-fry them until golden.

7   Tip the cooked crumb mixture over the salad.

8   Pour the vinegar into the pan, turn up the heat, and scrape the sediment in the pan with a wooden spoon to deglaze until almost all the vinegar has been boiled off.

9   Pour the pan juices over the salad. Season with pepper and toss lightly.

SMOKED SALMON SALAD

◑

Buy smoked salmon trimmings for this salad. Broil any pieces of skin you may find and snip them over the dressed salad.

This dressing is very rich, so we prefer to serve this salad as an appetizer.

1 EGG
10 OUNCES MIXED SALAD
    LEAVES
¼ POUND SMOKED SALMON
¼ CUP COTTAGE CHEESE
2 TSP GREEN PEPPERCORNS
1 LIME
½ LEMON
½ CUP LIGHT CREAM
SEA SALT AND FRESHLY GROUND
    BLACK PEPPER
SMALL BUNCH OF FRESH
    CHIVES, TO FINISH

1   Hard-boil the egg.

2   Meanwhile, wash and spin-dry the salad leaves. Tip them out on a large plate.

3   Snip the best pieces of salmon and set them aside for finishing.

4   In the food processor, whizz the remaining salmon with the cottage cheese and green peppercorns until smooth.

5   Zest and juice the lime and juice the lemon. Mix the lemon and lime juices together and set aside the lime zest.

6   Add the cream and fruit juices to the salmon and whizz again.

7   Peel the hard-boiled egg and chop roughly.

8   Add the chopped egg to the dressing. Season with salt and pepper.

9   Pour the dressing over the salad. Sprinkle with the reserved salmon pieces and lime zest and snip over the chives.

SMOKED TROUT AND DILL SALAD

●

¾ POUND MIXED SALAD LEAVES
4 SMOKED TROUT FILLETS
½ CUP CRÈME FRAÎCHE
1 TSP CREAM-STYLE
    HORSERADISH
1 TSP SWEET MUSTARD
SMALL BUNCH OF FRESH DILL
1 TBSP SUNFLOWER OIL
SEA SALT AND FRESHLY GROUND
    BLACK PEPPER

1   Wash and spin-dry the salad leaves and tip them out on a large plate.

2   Cut the trout fillets into thin strips and put them on top of the leaves.

3   In the food processor, whizz the crème fraîche with the horseradish, mustard, dill, and oil until smooth. Season with salt and pepper.

4   Pour the dressing over the salad.

Fish

The most important aspect of cooking fish in
10 minutes starts at the fish merchant's. Make
friends with him, and he will trim your
preparation time by cleaning, scaling,
trimming and filleting the fish when
you buy it.

Most supermarkets sell pre-wrapped fresh
dressed or drawn fish. These are relatively
expensive, but incredibly convenient.

To cook fresh fish fast, it is essential to use
small pieces. Remember, though, that it is all
too easy to overcook fish, particularly when
poaching: so keep the heat moderate and
poach very gently, so that the liquid is just
barely bubbling.

Steam-boiled Scallops (page 79)

POACHED SALMON CUTLETS WITH MANGO

●

This recipe is adapted from one created by Sri Owen, Britain's leading Indonesian food writer.

Allow 5-6 ounces salmon per person. Again we suggest using cutlets, as they are boneless and much easier to halve lengthwise.

Use a ripe – but still firm – mango and peel it Indian-style: cut off 2 pieces, one from either side of the pit, then peel off the skin from each piece.

2 TBSP OLIVE OIL
PIECE OF FRESH GINGERROOT, ABOUT 1 INCH ACROSS
2 SHALLOTS
1 GARLIC CLOVE
½ TSP CHILI POWDER
½ CUP WATER
1 TBSP WHITE WINE VINEGAR
1 TBSP ANCHOVY ESSENCE
1 TSP SUGAR
4 SALMON CUTLETS (PIECES OF FILLET)
SMALL BUNCH OF FRESH CILANTRO
1 LARGE MANGO

1 Heat the oil in a wok.

2 Peel the ginger, shallots, and garlic.

3 Whizz to a coarse paste in the food processor with the chili powder.

4 Add the paste to the wok and stir-fry 1 minute.

5 Pour in the water, vinegar, anchovy essence, and sugar and bring to a simmer.

6 Skin the salmon cutlets and divide each into 2 lengthwise. Add to the wok.

7 Snip in the cilantro leaves. Cook 3 minutes, turning the cutlets once. Take off the heat and leave in a warm place to settle 1-2 minutes.

8 Peel and chop the mango. Arrange the salmon on a warmed plate with the chopped mango and spoon over the cooking juices.

RED MULLET FILLETS WITH OLIVE AND TOMATO

●

Red mullet is rather time-consuming to fillet, so do ask your fishmonger to do it. Allow a good 6 ounces of fish per person.

As red mullet tend to be on the small side, you may prefer to cook them whole, but allow 1-2 minutes more cooking time on each side.

4 TBSP OLIVE OIL
3 RIPE TOMATOES
2 GARLIC CLOVES
6 PITTED RIPE OLIVES
2 SCALLIONS
2 TBSP TAPENADE (SEE PAGE 19)
SMALL BUNCHES OF FRESH HERBS TO INCLUDE: THYME, MARJORAM, AND PARSLEY
4-8 FILLETS OF RED MULLET (SEE ABOVE)
SEA SALT AND FRESHLY GROUND BLACK PEPPER.

1   Heat the broiler until very hot. Heat half the oil in a skillet.

2   In the food processor, whizz together the tomatoes, garlic, olives, and scallion.

3   Tip the mixture into the skillet and stir-fry 1 minute.

4   Add the tapenade and snip in the herbs.

5   Stir and simmer the mixture 5 minutes.

6   Meanwhile, paint the mullet fillets with the remaining oil.

7   Broil the fillets about 3 minutes on each side. The exact timing will depend on preference and the thickness of the fish.

8   Season and serve with the prepared sauce.

PAN-FRIED TUNA WITH FENNEL AND SUN-DRIED TOMATOES

●

Fresh tuna is meaty and strong-flavored and best bought as a steak about ¾ inch thick. Allow 5-6 ounces per person. If the steaks come from the middle of the fish, they will be very large and can be cut in 2 as required.

8 ANCHOVY FILLETS
2 GARLIC CLOVES
5 TBSP OLIVE OIL
4 TUNA STEAKS
2 TBSP CAPERS, DRAINED
⅔ CUP WHITE WINE
SMALL BUNCH OF FLAT-LEAF
   PARSLEY
SEA SALT AND FRESHLY GROUND
   BLACK PEPPER

1   Whizz the anchovies and garlic together in the food processor.

2   Heat half the oil in a skillet.

3   Add the anchovies and garlic and sweat them 2 minutes.

4   Add the fish and fry 3-4 minutes on each side. The exact timing will depend on preference and the thickness of the fish.

5   Remove the fish from the pan, put on a warmed plate, and keep warm.

6   Add the capers to the pan, pour in the rest of the oil and the wine. Snip in the parsley and season.

7   Stir over a high heat 1-2 minutes to reduce the sauce a little.

8   Season and pour the sauce over the fish.

FIVE-SPICE SEARED SALMON

●

If possible, buy salmon cutlets. These are fillets cut lengthwise as opposed to salmon steaks, which are cut across the fish. Look out for cutlets with the skin on, as the skin helps keep the flesh moist and has a good crispy texture when cooked. We generally allow one 5- to 6-ounce cutlet per person and broil it for about 4 minutes on each side.

PIECE OF FRESH GINGERROOT,
   ABOUT 1 INCH ACROSS
2 SCALLIONS
1 LEMON
1 TBSP FIVE-SPICE POWDER
1 TBSP SOY SAUCE
4 SALMON CUTLETS (PIECES OF
   FILLET)
SEA SALT

1 Heat the broiler until very hot.

2 Meanwhile, peel the ginger, put it in the food processor, and roughly snip the scallions in with it. Whizz to a thick paste.

3 Zest and juice the lemon. Add the lemon juice and zest, five-spice powder, and soy sauce to the paste along with salt to taste and whizz briefly.

4 Paste-paint the salmon with the mixture.

5 Broil the salmon, turning the cutlets over once, until evenly cooked. The exact timing will depend on preference and the thickness of the fish.

QUICK-MARINATED SMOKED HADDOCK

◗

*For this no-cook recipe, it is
essential to use lightly oak-smoked
undyed haddock (finnan haddie).*

1 POUND SMOKED HADDOCK
   (FINNAN HADDIE)
3 SCALLIONS
LARGE BUNCH OF FLAT-LEAF
   PARSLEY
1 LEMON
4 TBSP OLIVE OIL
FRESHLY GROUND BLACK
   PEPPER

1   Skin and bone the smoked
haddock.

2   Whizz in the food processor
until it is in coarse pieces. Tip the
prepared fish into a bowl.

3   Snip in the scallions and
parsley.

4   Zest and juice the lemon and
add the lemon zest and juice to the
bowl with the olive oil. Season with
black pepper.

5   Stir the mixture thoroughly and
let stand at least 10 minutes.

COD STEAKS WITH MUSTARD

●

*Buy cod steaks about $\frac{3}{4}$ inch thick
and allow 5 ounces per person.*

* As sometimes happens, the paste
may be on the stiff side: spread it
with a knife or spatula rather than
painting it on.*

2 SHALLOTS
1 SLICE OF DAY-OLD BREAD
SMALL BUNCH OF PARSLEY
2 TBSP COARSE-GRAIN MUSTARD
4 TBSP OLIVE OIL
4 COD STEAKS
2 TBSP BUTTER
4 TBSP LIGHT CREAM
3 TBSP WHITE WINE
SEA SALT AND FRESHLY GROUND
   BLACK PEPPER

1   Whizz the shallots, bread, and
parsley in the food processor.

2   Add half of the mustard and
half of the oil. Season and whizz
again to a thick coarse paste.

3   Paste-paint the cod with the
prepared mixture.

4   Heat the rest of the oil and
butter in a skillet.

5   Add the fish and fry over a
moderate heat 3-4 minutes on
each side.

6   Remove the fish from the pan,
put on a warmed plate, and keep
warm.

7   Swirl the cream and wine into
the pan along with the rest of the
mustard and season to taste.

8   Stir over a high heat 1 minute
to reduce the sauce a little, then
pour it over the fish.

STEAM-BOILED SCALLOPS

◐

Allow 1 or 2 medium-sized sea scallops per person and choose fresh scallops, ideally with plump brightly colored corals.

If good fish stock (homemade or purchased) is difficult to come by, use clam juice or water with a little extra sea salt and a dash of wine.

3 HEADS OF BELGIAN ENDIVE
1 ORANGE
4 TBSP BUTTER
3 TBSP FISH STOCK
6-8 SEA SCALLOPS,
    PREFERABLY WITH CORAL
2 TBSP NOILLY PRAT OR DRY
    VERMOUTH
SEA SALT AND FRESHLY GROUND
    BLACK PEPPER

1   Shred, rinse, and pat dry the endive.

2   Zest and juice the orange.

3   Melt half the butter in a wok, add the endive and sweat it 1-2 minutes.

4   Pour in the orange juice and fish stock.

5   Slice each scallop across horizontally into two disks. Put them on top of the endive with the orange zest.

6   Cover the pan tightly and steam-boil 2-3 minutes.

7   Using a slotted spoon, remove the scallops and endive from the wok, put on a warmed plate, season to taste, and keep warm.

8   Pour in the Noilly Prat or vermouth, turn up the heat, and reduce the sauce 1 minute.

9   Cut the rest of the butter into small pieces and whisk them into the sauce. Season and pour the finished sauce over the scallops.

JUMBO SHRIMP WITH CORIANDER

4 RAW JUMBO SHRIMP IN THEIR
   SHELLS
PIECE OF FRESH GINGERROOT,
   ABOUT ½ INCH ACROSS
1 GARLIC CLOVE
1 TSP GROUND CORIANDER
1 TSP PAPRIKA
1 TSP GROUND CUMIN
PINCH OF CAYENNE
3 TBSP WATER
1 TBSP VINEGAR
JUICE OF ½ LEMON
2 TBSP SUNFLOWER OIL

1   Rinse the unshelled shrimp and pat them dry, then trim off their heads and feet.

2   Peel the ginger and garlic.

3   Whizz them in the food processor with the coriander, paprika, cumin, and cayenne.

4   Add the water, vinegar, lemon juice, and half the oil. Whizz again until smooth.

5   Heat the rest of the oil in a wok.

6   Add the spice mixture and stir-fry 2-3 minutes over a moderate heat.

7   Add the shrimp and stir-fry 2 minutes.

FILLETS OF SOLE WITH ORANGE

●

We usually allow 6-ounce fillets per person and get our fishmonger to trim the fish for us.

If very small cook whole, but allow 1-2 minutes longer.

1 LEMON
2 ORANGES
½ CUP WHITE WINE
½ CUP WATER
8 FILLETS OF SOLE
4 TBSP HEAVY CREAM
BUNCH OF PARSLEY
SEA SALT AND FRESHLY GROUND
   BLACK PEPPER

1   Zest the lemon and juice both oranges and the lemon.

2   In a saucepan, bring to a boil the fruit juices, wine, water, and some sea salt. Reduce the heat and leave to simmer gently.

3   Cut the fillets of sole into 2-4 strips lengthwise, depending on size.

4   Add the strips of sole to the pan and poach 1-2 minutes, until just stiffened.

5   Using a slotted spoon, remove the sole from the pan. Put the fillets on a warmed plate and keep warm.

6   Turn up the heat and whisk the liquid until it is reduced by $\frac{1}{3}$.

7   Reduce the heat to low and stir in the cream and lemon zest.

8   Snip over the parsley, season, and pour the sauce over the sole.

Top: Jumbo Shrimp with Coriander; Bottom: grilled monkfish with Fennel and Sun-dried Tomato Sauce (page 87)

TROUT WITH LETTUCE

●

In spite of repeated pleas, even our friendliest of fishmongers draws the line at filleting trout. This means that there is no way that we can cook the fish in 10 minutes. Rather than leave it out altogether, however, we have included this favorite recipe on the grounds that the preparation time is minimal, even if the baking time does run to 20 minutes.

If time is not critical for this dish, excellent results are obtained by cooking the fish en papillote, *ie wrapped in a parcel of parchment paper or foil. The baking time then, however, should be about 20-25 minutes.*

½ HOTHOUSE CUCUMBER
2 HEADS OF ROMAINE LETTUCE
¼ POUND SORREL LEAVES
3 SCALLIONS
SMALL BUNCH OF PARSLEY
1 TSP CORIANDER SEEDS
4 TBSP BUTTER
4 SMALL TROUT, DRAWN
¾ CUP WHITE WINE
1 LEMON
SEA SALT AND FRESHLY GROUND
    BLACK PEPPER

1   Heat the oven to 375°F. Bring a saucepan of water to a boil.

2   Peel the cucumber and wash the vegetables.

3   Blanch 8 lettuce leaves in the boiling water 1 minute. Drain and pat dry.

4   In the food processor, whizz the rest of the lettuce with the sorrel, scallions, cucumber, parsley, coriander seeds, and seasoning to taste.

5   Use half the butter to grease a baking dish. Tip the mixture into the dish and spread it evenly over the bottom.

6   Season the insides of the trout and then wrap each in 2 of the blanched lettuce leaves.

7   Put the trout on top of the vegetable mixture. Pour over the white wine.

8   Juice the lemon and pour this over the trout, then dot with the remaining butter. Bake 15-20 minutes, depending on size.

9   With a pancake turner, transfer the fish to a dish. Season the vegetable mixture and spoon it over the trout.

FAST FISH SAUCES

As the simplest and fastest way of cooking fish is to grill, broil, poach, or fry it plainly, we like to prepare a fast sauce to go with it.

HOLLANDAISE SAUCES

Yes, you can make an excellent Hollandaise sauce in under 10 minutes! You must, however, have a food processor. Our Hollandaise sauces, and the Mousseline in particular, are well suited to the delicate texture and flavor of poached white fish.

1 BASIC HOLLANDAISE

In a small saucepan, boil 1 tablespoon of white wine vinegar and 4 tablespoons of water to reduce to about 1 tablespoon. Process 2 egg yolks until smooth, add the vinegar and whizz again briefly. Melt 10 tablespoons unsalted butter and trickle this into the mixture with the machine running. Process until the sauce thickens, then season to taste with salt and freshly ground black pepper.

2 TARRAGON HOLLANDAISE

Into a small saucepan, snip a handful of fresh tarragon leaves. Add 1 tablespoon of white wine vinegar and 4 tablespoons of water and reduce. Continue as for Basic Hollandaise as above.

3 TOMATO HOLLANDAISE

In a food processor, whizz a tomato and pour this into a cup. Rinse the bowl and make the Basic Hollandaise as above. Add the tomato purée to the sauce before final seasoning and whizz briefly to mix it in.

4 ORANGE HOLLANDAISE

Juice a blood orange. Make the Basic Hollandaise as above. Then, with the food processor running, trickle in the orange juice. Season to taste.

5 MOUSSELINE HOLLANDAISE

Whip $\frac{1}{4}$ cup whipping cream to just about soft peak. Make the Basic Hollandaise as above, then fold the cream into the finished sauce and season to taste.

BEURRE BLANC SAUCES

These classic sauces are surprisingly fast and simple. They suit most poached, broiled, grilled, or plainly baked fish.

1 BASIC BEURRE BLANC

In the food processor, whizz 2 shallots. In a small saucepan, simmer $\frac{2}{3}$ cup white wine with the chopped shallots until the mixture is soft and syrupy. Remove from the heat. Cut 1 stick unsalted butter into small pieces and whisk them into the pan, one piece at a time, until the sauce is smooth and shiny. Season lightly with sea salt and freshly ground black pepper.

2 BEURRE BLANC WITH ANCHOVY

In the food processor, whizz 2 shallots with 2 drained anchovy fillets. Make the Basic Beurre Blanc as above, using the shallot and anchovy mixture. Season lightly with freshly ground black pepper only.

3 BEURRE BLANC WITH MUSTARD

Make a Basic Beurre Blanc as above, but whisk in 1 tablespoon of Dijon mustard before adding the pieces of butter. Snip in a handful of fresh parsley. Season lightly.

CREAM SAUCES

As with all our other recipes for quick reduced sauces, remember to use a wide pan so that the liquid evaporates quickly.

1 SAFFRON CREAM SAUCE

Pour 4 tablespoons of white wine into a saucepan. Snip in a few strands of saffron. Simmer to reduce by about half. Stir in 1 cup whipping cream. Simmer, whisking occasionally, to reduce by about one-third. Beat in a pat of butter and season lightly with sea salt and freshly ground black pepper.

2 BASIL CREAM SAUCE

Pour 4 tablespoons of white wine into a saucepan. Simmer to reduce by about half. Stir in 1 cup whipping cream. Simmer, whisking occasionally, to reduce by about one-third. In the food processor, whizz a handful of fresh basil leaves to shred finely and beat them into the sauce with a pat of butter. Season lightly with sea salt and freshly ground black pepper.

3 CUCUMBER CREAM SAUCE

In the food processor, whizz a small peeled and seeded hothouse cucumber with a handful of fresh tarragon leaves. Melt a pat of butter in a saucepan and sweat the cucumber 1-2 minutes. Add 5 tablespoons of white wine and simmer until syrupy. Stir in 1 cup whipping cream. Simmer very gently, whisking occasionally, to reduce the sauce a little. Beat in a pat of butter and season with sea salt and freshly ground black pepper.

COMPOUND BUTTERS

Our no-cook butters should be made with unsalted butter as salted butter masks the taste and can spoil the delicate balance of flavor in a dish.

We serve these sauces to accompany firm-fleshed grilled or broiled fish. As a general rule the more robust the fish, the stronger flavor of butter it can take.

If you have the time, make a compound butter in advance, roll it into a sausage shape in a sheet of wax paper and chill for easy slicing into disks: otherwise, just paint or spread straight on the cooked fish.

These recipes are for 4 portions.

1 HERB BUTTER

In the food processor, whizz until smooth 4 tablespoons of butter with a few leaves of parsley, chives, chervil, and tarragon. Season with a little freshly ground black pepper.

2 ORANGE AND LEMON BUTTER

In the food processor, whizz a wedge each of a roughly chopped unpeeled orange and lemon to a purée. With the machine still running, add 4 tablespoons of butter then season with a little freshly ground black pepper.

3 WATERCRESS BUTTER

In the food processor, whizz until smooth a handful of watercress with 4 tablespoons of butter and a small pinch of sea salt.

4 GREEN PEPPERCORN BUTTER

In the food processor, whizz until smooth 2 teaspoons of drained green peppercorns with 4 tablespoons of butter and a small pinch of sea salt.

5 DILL AND HORSERADISH BUTTER

In the food processor, whizz until smooth 4 tablespoons of butter with a handful of fresh dill, 2 teaspoons of cream-style horseradish, and a little freshly ground black pepper.

6 MINT BUTTER

In the food processor, whizz until smooth 4 tablespoons of butter with a handful of fresh mint leaves and a little sea salt and freshly ground black pepper.

7 SMOKED SALMON BUTTER

In the food processor, whizz until smooth 6 tablespoons of butter with 1 ounce smoked salmon trimmings, 1 or 2 tablespoons of lemon juice, and a little freshly ground black pepper.

8 SHRIMP BUTTER

In the food processor, whizz until smooth 6 tablespoons of butter with 1 ounce well-drained peeled cooked shrimp, 1 teaspoon of anchovy essence, and a pinch of cayenne.

9 VERMOUTH BUTTER

In the food processor, whizz until smooth 6 tablespoons butter with a dash of dry vermouth and a little sea salt and freshly ground black pepper.

10 PERNOD BUTTER

In the food processor, whizz until smooth 6 tablespoons of butter with a dash of Pernod, a pinch of fennel seeds, and a little sea salt and freshly ground black pepper.

11 LIME BUTTER

In the food processor, whizz a coarsely chopped $\frac{1}{2}$ lime to a purée. With the machine still running, add 6 tablespoons butter and sea salt and freshly ground black pepper. Whizz until smooth.

12 CORIANDER BUTTER

In the food processor, whizz a handful of coriander seeds. With the machine still running, add 6 tablespoons butter and sea salt and freshly ground black pepper. Whizz until smooth.

OLIVE OIL SAUCES

The quality of the olive oil is obviously critical here, and we only ever use extra-virgin. As these sauces are rather gutsy, they go best with strong-flavored fish.

1 PARSLEY AND GARLIC SAUCE

In the food processor, whizz a handful of flat-leaf parsley, 1 garlic clove, and the juice of 1 lemon with a pinch each of sea salt and cayenne. With the machine running, trickle in $\frac{1}{2}$ cup olive oil. Process until thick and smooth.

2 FENNEL AND SUN-DRIED TOMATO SAUCE

In the food processor, coarsely shred $\frac{1}{2}$ a fennel bulb. Blanch 1 minute in boiling water then drain. Warm $\frac{1}{2}$ cup olive oil, add the fennel, and snip in 2 sun-dried tomatoes. Season with sea salt and freshly ground black pepper and stir well.

3 AVOCADO AND OLIVE SAUCE

In the food processor, process until smooth 1 peeled avocado with 2 garlic cloves, 6 pitted ripe olives, a dash of Tabasco, the juice of $\frac{1}{2}$ a lemon, and 3 tablespoons of red wine. Warm $\frac{2}{3}$ cup olive oil and stir in the mixture. Beat 1 egg yolk in a bowl and slowly whisk it into the warm mixture. Season with sea salt and freshly ground black pepper.

Meat and Poultry

In 10-minute cuisine, when it comes to meat and poultry we always opt for quality rather than quantity. The fact is that the more expensive cuts are the most tender. They are also usually well trimmed, they will need little preparation, and they will generally cook a great deal faster.

The most suitable 10-minute techniques for cooking meat and poultry are pan-frying, stir-frying, broiling, and grilling. The cooking method is dictated by the dish and the cut involved. For our purposes, pieces of meat and poultry should generally be no thinner than $\frac{1}{4}$ inch and no thicker than $\frac{3}{4}$ inch.

We tend to eat meat on the rare side – beef and lamb, in particular, we like pinkish. If you prefer your meat well done, you will obviously have to cook it slightly longer than the times we have given here.

Noisettes of Lamb with Tomatoes (page 97)

CORNISH HEN WITH HERBS AND OLIVES

●

When buying cornish hens, ask the butcher to spatchcock them: he will cut them along the backbone, then open them up and flatten them. The flatter the spatchcocked bird, the quicker it will cook: so, before paste-painting, flatten them still further using the heel of the hand or a rolling pin.

The meat of the hens is also scored deeply with a sharp knife to speed up the cooking process and allow the flavors of the paste to permeate.

To tell when the birds are cooked through, pierce the thickest piece of meat with the tip of the sharp knife – the juices should run clear.

8 GARLIC CLOVES
14 PITTED RIPE OLIVES
2 TBSP GROUND ALMONDS
HANDFUL EACH: THYME, MARJORAM, OREGANO, AND FLAT-LEAF PARSLEY
5 TBSP OLIVE OIL
SEA SALT AND FRESHLY GROUND BLACK PEPPER
2 CORNISH HENS

1   Heat the broiler until very hot.

2   In the food processor, whizz the garlic with the olives, almonds, and herbs.

3   Add the olive oil, season generously, and whizz again briefly to blend.

4   Using a sharp knife, deeply score the meat of the birds across several times.

5   Paste-paint the birds all over with the prepared mixture.

6   Broil the birds, turning them frequently, 8-10 minutes until brown and cooked through. Cut in half to serve.

CHICKEN WINGS WITH MARMALADE

◑

2 SCALLIONS
¼ CUP MARMALADE
2 TBSP OLIVE OIL
½ LEMON
8 CHICKEN WINGS
SEA SALT AND FRESHLY GROUND BLACK PEPPER

1   Heat the broiler until very hot.

2   In the food processor, whizz the scallions and then add the marmalade and oil. Whizz again to blend well.

3   Juice the lemon and add the juice to the mixture. Season the mixture and whizz again briefly.

4   Paste-paint the chicken wings with the prepared mixture.

5   Broil the chicken wings 6-8 minutes, turning them occasionally.

CHICKEN BREASTS WITH ZUCCHINI AND TARRAGON

●

3 ZUCCHINI
FEW SPRIGS OF TARRAGON
1 CUP CHICKEN STOCK
1 TBSP WHITE WINE VINEGAR
4 BONED CHICKEN BREAST
    HALVES
4 TBSP BUTTER
SEA SALT AND FRESHLY GROUND
    BLACK PEPPER

1   Roughly slice the zucchini and spread them evenly in a sauté pan. Sprinkle them with half the tarragon leaves.

2   Pour in the chicken stock and vinegar. Cover the pan and steam-boil the zucchini over a moderate heat for a couple of minutes.

3   Meanwhile, skin the chicken pieces and cut each in half lengthwise.

4   Place the chicken pieces over the zucchini, sprinkle with sea salt and the remaining tarragon leaves.

5   Cover and steam-boil 5 minutes.

6   Remove the chicken and zucchini from the pan, put them on a warmed plate, and keep warm.

7   Turn up the heat under the pan and whisk the butter into the cooking liquid. Season this sauce and pour it over the chicken.

CHICKEN WITH VERMOUTH AND SAGE

●

4 BONED CHICKEN BREAST
    HALVES
10 SAGE LEAVES
8 THIN SLICES OF PROSCIUTTO
1 TBSP OLIVE OIL
2 TBSP BUTTER
½ CUP DRY VERMOUTH
4 TBSP LIGHT CREAM
SEA SALT AND FRESHLY GROUND
    BLACK PEPPER

1   Skin the chicken pieces and cut each in half lengthwise.

2   Snip a couple of sage leaves over each piece of breast.

3   Wrap each piece in 2 slices of the prosciutto. If necessary, secure the parcels with a wooden toothpick.

4   Heat the oil with the butter in a sauté pan over a moderate heat.

5   Sauté the parcels 3-4 minutes on each side.

6   Pour in the vermouth and reduce the heat a little. Cover and cook a further 2-3 minutes.

7   Remove the chicken from the pan, place on a warmed dish, and keep warm.

8   Snip in the rest of sage and stir in the cream until heated through. Season the sauce and pour it over the chicken.

DUCK WITH CRANBERRY SAUCE

●

Boned duck breast halves are now sold in most supermarkets. If those you buy are very large, start off by cutting each diagonally across in half to end up with two portions, each weighing about 6 ounces. To speed up the cooking, using a very sharp knife, make 4 or 5 deep slanting cuts through the skin and into the meat.

If fresh cranberries are not available, use frozen ones instead and they will simply thaw as they are cooked.

1 CUP CRANBERRIES
2 TBSP SUGAR
2 TSP OLIVE OIL
4 DUCK BREAST HALVES
4 TBSP PORT WINE
SEA SALT AND FRESHLY GROUND
   BLACK PEPPER

1 Put the cranberries, sugar, and water to cover in a small saucepan.

2 Bring to a boil, reduce the heat, and simmer until the cranberries pop.

3 Heat the oil in a sauté pan.

4 Slit the skin and meat of the duck breast halves (see above) and season.

5 Sauté the duck – skin side down – 3-4 minutes. Turn the duck over and sauté a further 2-3 minutes. Occasionally press the pieces of duck down into the pan.

6 Using a slotted spoon, remove the duck from the pan, arrange on a warmed plate, and keep warm.

7 Tip out most of the fat from the pan.

8 Turn up the heat. Pour the port wine into the pan and scrape the pan with a wooden spoon to deglaze, until most of the alcohol has been driven off.

9 Stir in the cranberries, season the sauce, and pour it over the duck.

BLOOD SAUSAGE WITH APPLE

●

Some butchers still make their own blood sausage and these are usually worth buying. Otherwise, look out for fresh blood sausage rather than the pre-packed varieties. Cut them into slices about ½ inch thick, which will cook fast without collapsing.

As for the apples, we prefer to use varieties such as Granny Smith as they cook fast, hold their shape well and have a good depth of flavor.

3 TBSP BUTTER
2 APPLES
1 POUND BLOOD SAUSAGE
½ CUP DRY HARD CIDER
2 TSP DIJON MUSTARD
SEA SALT AND FRESHLY GROUND
    BLACK PEPPER

1 Melt two-thirds of the butter in a skillet.

2 Core the apples and then cut them into 8 slices.

3 Add the apples to the pan and fry them over a low heat, turning once.

4 Slice the blood sausage (see above).

5 Push the apples to the side of the pan and add the sausage.

6 Fry the sausage over a low heat 3-4 minutes on each side.

7 Using a slotted spoon, remove the sausage and apple from the pan, arrange them on a warmed plate, and keep warm.

8 Turn up the heat under the pan and pour in the cider.

9 Whisk in the rest of the butter along with the mustard. Scrape the pan well with a wooden spoon to deglaze. Season the sauce and pour it over the sausage.

Left: Chicken with Vermouth and Sage (page 91) on a bed of rice; Right: Blood Sausage with Apple.

CALVES' LIVER WITH RAISINS

●

No matter how thin the butcher usually slices calves' liver, ask him to slice it even thinner (ideally, it should be paper-thin) and allow about 5 ounces per person. Use a large skillet and cook the liver very fast so that it is seared on the outside but still remains pink inside.

1 TBSP RED WINE VINEGAR
1 TBSP WATER
1 TSP SUGAR
3 TBSP RAISINS
4 SAGE LEAVES
3 TBSP BUTTER
4 SLICES CALVES' LIVER
SEA SALT AND FRESHLY GROUND
    BLACK PEPPER

1   Heat the vinegar, water, sugar, raisins, and 2 sage leaves in a small saucepan until the liquid is boiling.

2   Reduce the heat and simmer 1 minute, then season.

3   Melt the butter with the rest of the sage in a large skillet. Add the liver and sauté over a moderate-to-high heat 1 minute on each side.

4   Quickly remove the liver from the pan, put it on a warmed plate, season, and keep warm.

5   Pour the vinegar mixture into the pan and turn up the heat a little.

6   Using a wooden spoon, scrape the pan to deglaze and drive off most of the vinegar. Pour the sauce over the liver.

CHICKEN LIVERS WITH ORANGE

◑

For this dish, we prefer to use a slightly sweet sherry – amontillado or, better still, oloroso. Both combine well with the orange.

½ POUND CHICKEN LIVERS
1 GARLIC CLOVE
½ ORANGE
1 TBSP OLIVE OIL
2 TBSP BUTTER
2 TBSP SHERRY
FEW SPRIGS OF MARJORAM
SEA SALT AND FRESHLY GROUND
    BLACK PEPPER

1   Trim and slice the chicken livers. Rinse and pat them dry.

2   Chop the garlic.

3   Zest and juice the orange.

4   Heat the oil and butter in a sauté pan. Add the livers and garlic and sauté them a few minutes – the exact timing will depend on how pink the livers are to be – turning from time to time.

5   Add the sherry, orange zest and juice and snip in the marjoram.

6   Season and stir 1 minute before serving.

NOISETTES OF LAMB WITH TOMATOES

●

If you cannot find small noisettes of lamb weighing 2-3 ounces (and no more than about ¾ inch thick), use lamb steaks instead (trimming off all their visible fat and cooking them 1 or 2 minutes longer).

The more fresh herbs used, the more pungent the sauce. If you are not entirely sure about the sweetness of the tomatoes, add a pinch of sugar.

3 RIPE TOMATOES
2 GARLIC CLOVES
FEW SPRIGS EACH OF:
    OREGANO, THYME, MARJORAM
    AND ROSEMARY
2 TBSP OLIVE OIL
3 TBSP WHITE WINE
8 NOISETTES OF LAMB
SEA SALT AND FRESHLY GROUND
    BLACK PEPPER
1 LEMON, TO SERVE

1 Whizz the tomatoes with the garlic and herbs.

2 Heat the oil in a sauté pan. Add 2 tablespoons of the prepared mixture and cook over a moderate heat 1 minute or so.

3 Turn up the heat to high, season the noisettes and put them in the pan on top of the mixture. Cook them 2-3 minutes on each side.

4 Remove the noisettes from the pan and put aside to keep warm.

5 Add the remaining mixture to the pan, reduce the heat to moderate, and cook a minute or two.

6 Add the wine and stir 1 minute.

7 Cut the lemon into quarters and serve to accompany the meat dressed with the pan juices.

LAMB CHOPS WITH GINGER

●

Although expensive, lamb rib chops are lean, tender, and cook very fast. As they tend to be rather small, we suggest 2 chops per person.

A low-fat yogurt, unless slowly stirred into the sauce, is likely to curdle: so use a full-fat thick yogurt, preferably made from sheep's milk.

PIECE OF FRESH GINGERROOT,
    1 INCH ACROSS
1 GARLIC CLOVE
2 SCALLIONS
1 STALK OF FRESH LEMON
    GRASS
1 TBSP CHILI OIL
8 LAMB RIB CHOPS
4 TBSP WHITE WINE
4 TBSP THICK PLAIN YOGURT
SEA SALT AND FRESHLY GROUND
    BLACK PEPPER

1 In the food processor, whizz the ginger with the garlic, scallion, lemon grass, sea salt to taste, and half of the chili oil.

2 Paste-paint the lamb chops with the prepared mixture.

3 Heat the rest of the chili oil in a sauté pan. Add the chops to the pan and sauté them 3 minutes on each side.

4 Remove the meat from the pan, put on a warmed dish, and keep warm.

5 Pour the wine and yogurt into the pan and stir over a low heat 1 minute.

6 Season the sauce and the lamb lightly, then pour the sauce over the meat.

STRIPS

The more tender cuts of beef, veal, pork, and chicken cook very fast indeed when cut into thin strips. Start off with slices about $\frac{1}{4}$ inch thick, then cut them across (preferably along the grain, for minimum shrinkage and maximum texture) into pieces about 2-3 inches long and 1 inch wide. A wok – with its deep sides and rounded base – is the ideal pan for cooking such strips. Make sure the cooking medium is hot enough to seize and seal the meat as soon as it hits the pan.

1 CHICKEN STRIPS WITH SESAME SEEDS

Cut 1 pound of boned and skinned chicken breast into strips. Heat 1 tablespoon of oil in a wok. Stir-fry a handful of sesame seeds with 1-2 snipped scallions 1 minute. Add the chicken strips and stir-fry 1-2 minutes. Stir in 1 tablespoon of soy sauce and a few drops of chili sauce. Snip in a few leaves of fresh cilantro and sprinkle in a dash of sesame oil. Season with sea salt and freshly ground black pepper and serve.

2 VEAL STRIPS WITH LEMON

Cut 1 pound of veal cutlets into strips. Heat about $\frac{1}{2}$ cup of a light (veal, chicken, or vegetable) stock in a wok. Poach the veal gently in the stock along with a handful of tarragon leaves, a few green peppercorns, and the zest of a lemon a couple of minutes. Using a slotted spoon, remove the veal from the pan. Turn up the heat to reduce the stock a little. Add 3 tablespoons of thick yogurt, a dash of lemon juice, and a pinch of sugar. Tip the veal strips back in, stir together, season with sea salt and freshly ground black pepper, and serve.

3 PORK STRIPS WITH SHIITAKE MUSHROOMS

Cut 1 pound of pork tenderloin into strips. Heat 2 tablespoons of oil in a wok. Stir-fry the pork with a minced garlic clove and a little chopped fresh gingerroot. Slice $\frac{1}{2}$ handful of fresh shiitake mushrooms and add them to the wok with some snow peas and 1 tablespoon of plum sauce. Stir-fry a couple of minutes, sprinkle in a dash of dry sherry, season with sea salt and freshly ground black pepper, and serve.

4 10-MINUTE STROGANOFF

Cut 1 pound of filet mignon into strips and sprinkle them generously with paprika. Heat 1 tablespoon of oil and a pat of butter in a wok over a high heat. Stir-fry the beef along with a couple of snipped scallions a couple of minutes and remove with a slotted spoon. Pour out the fat. Over a low heat, swirl in 1-2 tablespoons of brandy, 1 teaspoon of tomato ketchup, a dash of lemon juice, and $\frac{3}{4}$ cup of sour cream. Simmer a minute or two, tip the beef strips back in, and stir together. Season with sea salt and freshly ground black pepper and serve.

10-minute Stroganoff with Basic Butter Noodles (page 106)

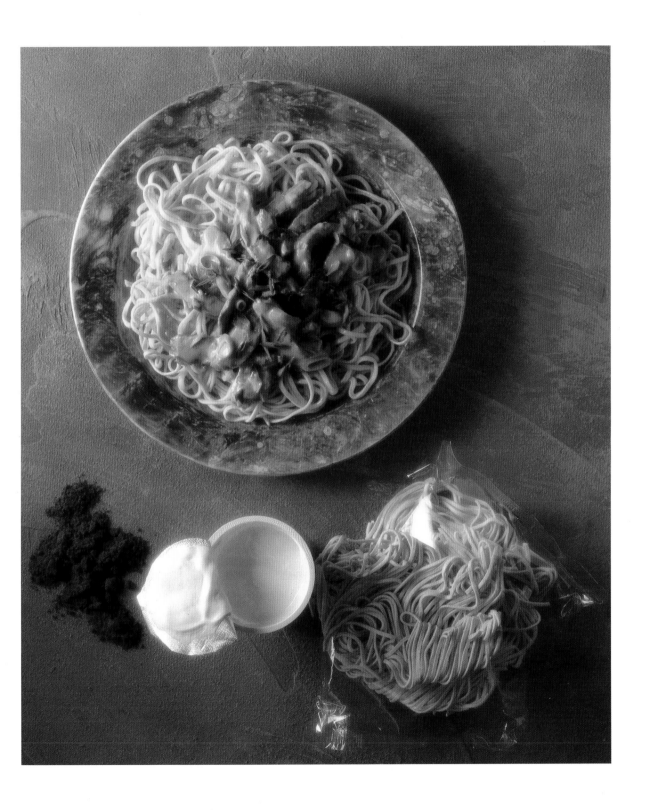

10-MINUTE HAMBURGERS

Even before the recent worries about the wisdom of eating beef, we never bought ready-ground beef, preferring to whizz our own from lean steak. When doing this, be very careful not to over-process as this ruins the texture and makes the burger far too heavy and dense.

The ideal weight for fast-cooking burgers is about 2½ ounces and the fastest way to shape them is to take roughly the right amount of beef between the palms of the hands, roll it into a round ball and then flatten this into a patty. The fastest means of cooking hamburgers is either to broil, grill or pan-fry them, making sure that the element, coals or pan is thoroughly heated beforehand. Allow 2 per person.

1 BASIC HAMBURGER

Whizz 10 ounces trimmed and roughly chopped steak with 1 scallion, 1 egg, 1 teaspoon of mustard, and a dash each of tomato paste, Worcestershire sauce and Tabasco. Season well with sea salt and freshly ground black pepper. Make into 4 patties.

2 SPICED HAMBURGER

Whizz 10 ounces trimmed and roughly chopped steak with 1-2 scallions, 2 teaspoons of harissa (or chili sauce) and a pinch each of ground cumin, coriander, and cinnamon. Season with sea salt and freshly ground black pepper.

3 HERB HAMBURGER

Whizz 10 ounces trimmed and roughly chopped steak with 1 garlic clove, 1 teaspoon of Dijon mustard, and a handful each of: parsley, summer savory, thyme, and rosemary. Season with sea salt and freshly ground black pepper.

4 CHILI HAMBURGER

Whizz 10 ounces trimmed and roughly chopped steak with a garlic clove, 1 teaspoon each of chili and soy sauces, and a dash of anchovy essence. Season with sea salt and freshly ground black pepper.

GRILLED MEAT & POULTRY

The most obvious and simplest way of cooking meat and poultry fast is to grill or broil it. For this treatment it is particularly important to buy top-quality produce. Despite their size, whole pieces of meat actually cook just as fast as kebabs, which are fiddly and time-consuming to skewer on sticks.

We always choose finely trimmed cuts with the minimum of visible fat. Unfortunately, these types of cut — fillets, tenderloins, rib chops, and noisettes, for example — are the most expensive. Pieces of meat and poultry for grilling should be about $\frac{1}{2}$-$\frac{3}{4}$ inch thick, and we usually allow about 4-6 ounces per person. Grilled meat and poultry are best either paste-painted before grilling or served with a compound butter (see below).

PASTE-PAINTS

As we have already mentioned on page 31, paste-painting is 10-minute cuisine's answer to marinating. As the meat or poultry grills, the paste holds in the flavor and creates a crust which adds extra taste and texture.

Most of these mixtures may also be served as side-sauces to accompany plainly grilled or broiled meat and poultry.

1 CORIANDER AND CUMIN

Mix 1 teaspoon each of ground coriander and cumin with a dash of harissa (or chili sauce), the juice of 1 lime, sea salt and freshly ground black pepper, and 4 tablespoons of thick plain yogurt. Good with lamb.

2 YOGURT AND MINT

In the food processor, whizz 4 tablespoons of thick plain yogurt with a handful of mint leaves, 1 garlic clove, a pinch each of ground turmeric, cumin, and coriander, and sea salt and freshly ground black pepper. Good with lamb or chicken.

3 HONEY AND MUSTARD

Mix together 1 tablespoon of runny honey with 1 tablespoon of coarse-grain mustard, 2 teaspoons of tomato paste and 2 tablespoons of olive oil. Season lightly with sea salt and freshly ground black pepper. Good with all poultry.

4 ORANGE AND PORT WINE

In the food processor, whizz $\frac{1}{4}$ of a roughly chopped unpeeled orange to a purée. Whizz in a handful of thyme and parsley and 2 teaspoons each of port wine, red currant jelly, and olive oil. Good with venison.

5 BLUE CHEESE

Whizz 3 ounces blue cheese with a garlic clove, 2 teaspoons of brandy, and 1 tablespoon of olive oil until smooth. Season with freshly ground black pepper. Good with steaks.

COMPOUND BUTTERS

Make these with unsalted butter, and see page 86 for the fast and simple technique for preparing them.

1 ORANGE AND HERB BUTTER

In the food processor, whizz a wedge of a roughly chopped unpeeled orange to a purée. With the machine still running, add 4 tablespoons of butter, 1-2 sage leaves, and several sprigs each of rosemary, chives, and parsley. Season with sea salt and freshly ground black pepper. Good with beef and chicken.

2 BRANDY AND PEPPER BUTTER

In the food processor, whizz until smooth 4 tablespoons of butter with 1 tablespoon of brandy, a few black peppercorns, 1 teaspoon of Dijon mustard, and a few leaves of parsley. Good with beef.

3 MUSHROOM BUTTER

In the food processor, whizz until smooth 4 tablespoons butter with a few mushrooms, 1 scallion, a dash of sherry, and a pinch of cayenne. Good with beef and poultry.

4 SHALLOT AND TOMATO BUTTER

In the food processor, whizz until smooth 1 small ripe tomato with 2 shallots, a few sprigs of parsley, a dash of lemon juice and 4 tablespoons butter. Season with sea salt and freshly ground black pepper. Good with steaks.

Vegetables, Noodles and Rice

In 10-minute cuisine there is really not a great deal of time for vegetables and other accompaniments – and, in any case, we always serve a salad!

For these reasons we keep our vegetables, rice, and noodles relatively simple. Since there is often no time to prepare separate dishes, one good trick is to combine them and to cook vegetables along with rice or noodles.

Grilled vegetables (page 105)

VEGETABLES

It will come as no surprise to learn that here, as everywhere else, we use only fresh vegetables (the only possible exceptions are frozen spinach and cans of petits pois).

We have 3 basic techniques for cooking vegetables in 10 minutes:

Grilled chicken breast half paste-painted with Honey and Mustard (page 101) and served with steam-boiled broccoli and snow peas

STEAM-BOILING

As you would expect, this is a mixture of steaming and boiling and incorporates the best aspects of both techniques. As with steaming, the true taste, texture, and most of the nutrients of the vegetables are maintained, but this is achieved with the speed of boiling.

The only equipment needed is a good wide-bottomed saucepan with a tight-fitting lid. Into this, put just enough lightly salted boiling water to cover the bottom. Then tip in the vegetables, cover, and boil over a high heat a couple of minutes (for crunchy vegetables) or until cooked as preferred. To check whether the vegetables are done, lift the lid and test for texture with the point of a sharp knife. Once cooked, drain the vegetables thoroughly and season.

Tiny baby vegetables, such as carrots, baby corn, zucchini, asparagus, cherry tomatoes, snow peas, and green beans can be cooked whole. Otherwise, slice, chop, sliver, or shred them. The ideal size varies with the vegetable.

Cauliflower and broccoli are best broken into tiny florets no larger than 1 inch. Larger carrots and zucchini, celery, and leeks can either be cut into 1-inch slices or shredded (see page 30). Keep the tips of large, thick asparagus whole; the stalks, like string beans, cook faster when slivered (see page 30).

The quickest (if slightly wasteful) way of preparing fine green beans is to grab a handful, knock them on a work surface to align the tops, snip off those tops, turn them over, bang again to align the tails, and snip these off. If the beans are still too long, snip them across in half.

BROILING

Broiled vegetables are delicious – with robust textures and tastes – and their slightly burnt, charred flavor is a great joy.

To prepare them for broiling, slice vegetables in half lengthwise (and in half again, if they are very big!). Then paint them lightly all over with olive oil and sprinkle them with sea salt.

Heat the broiler or barbecue until very hot and cook the vegetables for a few minutes on each side until just soft and tender. Do not worry if they look slightly charred: it only improves their flavor.

Most Mediterranean vegetables are ideal for this treatment. Sadly, not all of them cook fast enough – but the ones that suit our purposes include zucchini, sweet peppers, onions, fennel, chicories (including radicchio), and tomatoes.

SAUTÉING OR STIR-FRYING

What you call this method depends really on whether a wok or a sauté pan is being used. As with steam-boiling, all but the tiniest vegetables must be trimmed to a suitable size.

Whichever pan is being used, heat just enough oil, butter (butter on its own does tend to blacken and burn), or a mixture of both, to coat the bottom of the pan and tip in the prepared vegetables. Stir them over a moderate heat until they are cooked to taste – it probably will not be more than about 3 minutes – and season.

Whole button or sliced larger mushrooms, baby corn, snow peas, green peas, shredded spinach or lettuce leaves, slivered cucumbers or zucchini and bean sprouts are all quick to prepare and sauté or stir-fry well.

NOODLES

We eat noodles – both Italian and Oriental varieties – with most of our meat and fish dishes.

According to Yan-Kit So, the well-known Chinese food writer, there are over 500 types of Oriental noodle, all made with different ingredients or in various shapes.

For this reason, do not just rely on the small selection of noodles available in your local supermarket. Be adventurous – raid an Oriental grocers and stock up with as many kinds as appeal to you! Look out for beanthread or cellophane, egg, wheat, rice-flour, and shrimp- and other flavored noodles. As they are so cheap, if they don't go down well it will not have been an expensive mistake.

BASIC WAYS OF COOKING NOODLES

Always follow the instructions on the package. Generally speaking, beanthread noodles are simply soaked in very hot water for a few minutes until soft. They are then drained and chopped to a manageable size.

For wheat or egg noodles, cook them in boiling salted water 3-4 minutes until soft. Then drain, refresh, separate them, and drain them again, if necessary.

Once cooked, noodles can be finished in different ways:

1 BASIC BUTTER NOODLES

Prepare the noodles as described on the previous page. Stir in a pat of butter. Season with sea salt and freshly ground black pepper.

2 BASIC OIL NOODLES

Prepare the noodles as above. Stir in 1 tablespoon of oil and season. The oil you use will depend on the main dish: for a strong flavor, add a few drops of sesame oil: for a milder flavor, plain peanut or sunflower oil is preferable.

3 HERB NOODLES

Prepare the noodles as above, finishing with either butter or oil. Snip in a handful of chives, flat-leaf parsley, or chervil.

TWICE-COOKED NOODLES

Twice-cooking is a traditional Chinese two-step technique, often involving first simmering then stir-frying. We use it to add flavor, interest, and bite to plain noodles and most of the twice-cooked noodle dishes below, in sufficient quantity, make ideal 10-minute snacks or simple meals in themselves.

1 MUSHROOM NOODLES

In a wok, heat 1 tablespoon of olive oil. Add a few sliced oyster mushrooms and stir-fry 1-2 minutes. Add the prepared noodles (see above) and stir-fry until heated through. Season with sea salt and freshly ground black pepper.

2 SNOW PEA NOODLES

In a wok, heat 1 tablespoon of olive oil. Snip in a scallion and a handful of snow peas. Stir-fry 1-2 minutes. Add the prepared noodles (see above) and stir-fry until heated through. Season with sea salt and freshly ground black pepper.

Snow Pea Noodles

3 LEEK NOODLES

In a wok, heat 1 tablespoon of olive oil. Add 1 shredded leek and a pinch of thyme and stir-fry 1-2 minutes. Add the prepared noodles (see above) and stir-fry until heated through. Season with sea salt and freshly ground black pepper.

4 SUN-DRIED TOMATO NOODLES

In a wok, heat 1 tablespoon of the oil from sun-dried tomatoes. Snip in a couple of sun-dried tomatoes and stir-fry 1 minute. Add the prepared noodles (see above). Snip in a few basil leaves and stir-fry until heated through. Season with sea salt and freshly ground black pepper.

5 ALMOND NOODLES

In a wok, heat 1 tablespoon of olive oil. Add a handful of almond slivers and stir-fry 1-2 minutes. Add the prepared noodles (see above) and stir-fry until heated through. Season with sea salt and freshly ground black pepper.

6 ROASTED GARLIC NOODLES

In a wok, heat 1 tablespoon of the oil from roasted garlic. Add a couple of the roasted cloves, mash and stir-fry 1-2 minutes. Add the prepared noodles (see above), snip in a handful of flat-leaf parsley, and stir-fry until heated through. Season with sea salt and freshly ground black pepper.

7 CHILI NOODLES 1

In a wok, heat 1 tablespoon of oil. Snip in a couple of scallions and add a pinch of chili powder. Add the prepared noodles (see above) and stir-fry 1-2 minutes. Sprinkle over a few drops of soy sauce.

8 CHILI NOODLES 2

In a wok, heat 1 tablespoon of oil. Add a couple of dried chilis and stir-fry 2-3 minutes. Add the prepared noodles (see above) and stir-fry until heated through. Season.

RICE

Sadly, the more interesting varieties of rice (brown, basmati, arborio) have to be avoided by the 10-minute cook on the grounds that they take far too long.

What we have found, however, is that partially-cooked instant rice works very well, especially if flavored with some of our Bits and Pieces for Rice (see below).

COOKING RICE

Always follow the instructions on the package. Generally speaking, rice will taste much better if it is cooked in stock rather than water. This works better still if the stock complements the main dish: for example, if you are serving chicken and have either chicken or vegetable stock handy, use it to cook the rice.

BITS & PIECES FOR RICE

1   Mix a couple of cinnamon sticks with the rice and boil them together.

2   Mix a couple of bay leaves with the rice and boil them together.

3   Mix a few sprigs of thyme with the rice and boil them together.

4   Mix a few dried wild mushrooms with the rice and boil them together.

5   While the rice is simmering, throw in a handful of pine nuts.

6   While the rice is simmering, add a few sliced mushrooms and a pat of butter.

7   While the rice is simmering, add a pinch of powdered saffron and a pat of butter.

8   While the rice is simmering, add a few sprigs of tarragon, a dash of white wine vinegar, and a pat of butter.

9   Once the rice is cooked, stir in a pat of Orange and Lemon butter (see page 86).

10   Once the rice is cooked, stir in some shredded Cheddar and a pat of butter.

11   Once the rice is cooked, snip in some chives and chervil and stir in a pat of butter.

12   Once the rice is cooked, stir in 1-2 tablespoons of olive oil and a dash of vinegar.

Last Courses

Fresh fruit is one of the easiest and most satisfying ways to finish off any meal: the other is a selection of good cheeses. However, some people feel very deprived without a proper dessert; so for all those with a sweet tooth we have happily concocted some 10-minute last courses.

Frosted fruit (page 112)

FRESH FRUIT

Use whatever fruits are in season, choosing for taste, color, and shape.

Most fruits look more appealing left on their stalks or with their leaves intact – particularly berries and citrus fruits.

Make a fuss of your fruit and, for a sumptuous show, arrange it as a table centerpiece on a dish or flat-sided bowl, piling the fruit high in a generous mound and letting some hang over the sides. Alternatively, just place them on the table amid a bed of ivy or fresh grape leaves.

In among the fruit, tuck: sprigs of mint and other edible leaves; miniature cookies, such as florentines, amaretti, and cantucci; sweets, such as slices of panforte, nougat, candied fruit, and mint crisps; or even dried and crystallized fruit, such as figs, apricots, dates, and prunes.

FROSTED FRUIT

SEASONAL FRUIT: SUCH AS
    STRAWBERRIES, GRAPES,
    RED, WHITE OR BLACK
    CURRANTS, TANGERINES,
    APPLES, ETC
LEMONS, AS REQUIRED
CONFECTIONERS' SUGAR, AS
    REQUIRED

1   Wash the fruit and pat it dry.

2   If using larger fruit, cut it into bite-sized pieces and sprinkle with lemon juice to prevent discoloration.

3   Arrange the fruit on a plate (see above).

4   Sift confectioners' sugar over it until it is all covered with a light film.

5   Chill the dusted fruit while the rest of the meal is in progress, and serve straight from the refrigerator.

PEACHES WITH AMARETTI

Look out for white peaches as they have an incredibly intense flavor. There is no need to peel them, simply wipe them clean. It is much quicker and cheaper to buy amaretti unwrapped in packages, rather than buying the individually wrapped type.

4 WHITE PEACHES
2 OUNCES AMARETTI COOKIES
3 TBSP BUTTER

1   Heat the oven to 375°F.

2   Wash, pat dry, halve, and pit the peaches. Arrange in a gratin dish.

3   In a food processor, whizz the cookies to crumbs and scatter these over the peaches.

4   Dot the crumbs with butter and bake in the oven 7 minutes.

5   Finish by browning the topping briefly under a very hot broiler.

PAN-FRIED APPLE SLICES

We prefer to use apples such as Granny Smith, as they cook faster, have a better flavor and retain their shape and texture.

4 APPLES
4 TBSP UNSALTED BUTTER
2 TBSP RAISINS IN SCOTCH (SEE
    CABINET SAUCES, PAGE 18)
2 TBSP SYRUP FROM THE
    RAISINS IN SCOTCH (SEE
    ABOVE)
1 TBSP RUNNY HONEY
CRÈME FRAÎCHE OR THICK
    PLAIN YOGURT, TO SERVE

1   Wash, pat dry, quarter, and core the apples. Cut each quarter again in half.

2   Melt the butter in a skillet.

3   Add the apple slices and sauté them gently 3-5 minutes.

4   Remove the apples from the pan with a slotted spoon and put on a warmed dish.

5   Pour the raisins and their syrup into the pan.

6   Stir in the honey and simmer 1 minute.

7   Pour the mixture over the cooked apples. Serve with crème fraîche or thick yogurt.

BAKED BANANAS

Overripe bananas will collapse into a mush, so use only firm fruit for this recipe.

4 BANANAS
6 TBSP APRICOT JAM
2 TBSP VODKA
SMALL HANDFUL OF MINT
  LEAVES
2 TBSP UNSALTED BUTTER

1   Heat the oven to 425°F.

2   Peel and split the bananas lengthwise.

3   Put each banana half on a piece of foil large enough to be able to wrap it generously.

4   In a small bowl, mix the apricot jam with the vodka and snip in the mint leaves.

5   Paste-paint each banana with the mixture, dot with butter, and wrap the foil around the bananas to make individual packages.

6   Bake the banana packages 10 minutes.

FRUIT GRATIN

This combination of plums and Mascarpone is our favorite fruit gratin. However, any fruit can be used, and Mascarpone can be replaced by heavy cream or crème fraîche.

8 PLUMS
¼ CUP MASCARPONE
4 TBSP SUGAR

1   Heat the broiler.

2   Wash, pat dry, halve, and pit the plums. Put in a gratin dish.

3   Dollop the mascarpone over the plums and sprinkle them with the sugar.

4   Broil until caramelized.

FRUIT SKEWERS

Most kebabs are a waste of time for the 10-minute cook, but these fruit skewers are worth a few precious moments. Use firm-textured fruit which will not collapse: whole strawberries and grapes; halved apricots, figs, and plums; slices of pear and apple; segments of orange, grapefruit, tangerine and mandarin; and chunks of pineapple.

Thread the prepared fruit on skewers. If you are leaving them while you prepare the first course, sprinkle them with lemon juice so that they do not discolor.

Just before cooking, paste-paint them with one of the sweet butters described overleaf. Broil about 1 minute on each side, just enough to melt the butter and heat the fruit through.

SWEET BUTTERS

1 RUM BUTTER

In the food processor, whizz until smooth 4 tablespoons unsalted butter with 1 tablespoon of rum and 1 tablespoon of brown sugar. Good with pineapple.

2 COINTREAU BUTTER

In the food processor, whizz until smooth 4 tablespoons unsalted butter with 1 tablespoon of Cointreau and 1 tablespoon of confectioners' sugar. Good with orange or grapefruit.

3 AMARETTO BUTTER

In the food processor, whizz 4 tablespoons unsalted butter with 1 tablespoon amaretto liqueur and a couple of amaretti cookies. Good with plums.

4 BRANDY BUTTER

In the food processor, whizz until smooth 4 tablespoons unsalted butter with 2 tablespoons of brandy and 1 tablespoon of brown sugar. Good with apricots.

5 SCOTCH BUTTER

In the food processor, whizz until smooth 4 tablespoons unsalted butter with 1 tablespoon of Scotch, a small piece of crystallized ginger, and 1 tablespoon of confectioners' sugar. Good with strawberries or oranges.

6 GIN BUTTER

In the food processor, whizz 4 tablespoons unsalted butter with 1 tablespoon of gin, 1 tablespoon of confectioners' sugar, and a pinch of ground, almonds. Good with plums.

FRUITS IN ALCOHOL

Fruit steeped in alcohol is an effortless – but impressive – last course. Use ripe fruit and carefully match it to the alcohol, then simply leave it to macerate while the meal is in progress.

1 PEACHES IN ROSÉ WINE

Cut 4 ripe peaches in half. Pit and cut them in half again. Put the prepared slices into 4 large wine glasses and pour over enough good Loire rosé to cover them. Chill.

2 STRAWBERRIES WITH KIRSCH

Wipe and hull 1 pound (1½ pints) strawberries. Put them in a bowl and sprinkle with 2 tablespoons of Kirsch and a handful of mint leaves. Chill and serve with a bowl of thick set (Swiss style) yogurt beaten with confectioners' sugar to taste.

3 STRAWBERRIES WITH COINTREAU

Wipe and hull 1 pound (1½ pints) strawberries. Put them in a bowl and sprinkle with 2 tablespoons of Cointreau, along with the zest and juice of 1 orange. Chill.

4 MELON WITH MUSCAT

Halve and scoop out the seeds from 2 cantaloupes or other small melons. Cut a slice off the base of each half so that they lie flat, then pour into each 2-3 tablespoons of Muscat de Beaumes de Venise, Orange Muscat, or any heavily scented honeyed dessert wine. Chill.

5 GRAPES WITH KIRSCH

Mix together a generous 1 pound seedless grapes with $\frac{2}{3}$ cup of crème fraîche, a sprinkling of brown sugar, and 3 tablespoons of Kirsch. Chill.

FRUIT FOOLS

Choose very ripe fruit and serve with amaretti cookies, brandy snaps or any good tiny bought cookies.

1 MANGO AND LIME FOOL

In a food processor, whizz 1 ripe peeled and chopped mango with $\frac{1}{4}$ of a fresh lime. Add 3 tablespoons of thick plain yogurt and 1 tablespoon of heavy cream and whizz again briefly. Sweeten to taste with confectioners' sugar.

2 RASPBERRY AND LEMON BALM FOOL

In a food processor, whizz 1 pound (2 pints) ripe raspberries with a handful of lemon balm leaves and a dash of Cassis. (If time allows, strain the seeds out at this stage.) Add 4 tablespoons of heavy cream and whizz again briefly. Sweeten to taste with confectioners' sugar.

Raspberry and Lemon Balm Fool

ICE-CREAM

There is nothing wrong with using a bought ice-cream, provided it is a good one. We both like vanilla flavor and find that it works best with our sweet sauces.

ICE-CREAM SAUCES

1 HOT APRICOT SAUCE

Melt 2 tablespoons unsalted butter in a skillet. Stir in a handful of chopped hazelnuts and brown briefly. Stir in $\frac{1}{4}$ cup of apricot jam and a dash of sweet wine. Simmer a couple of minutes.

2 HOT MARMALADE SAUCE

In a saucepan, heat together $\frac{1}{4}$ cup of marmalade with 1 tablespoon of scotch until just bubbling.

3 WALNUT AND HONEY SAUCE

Melt 2 tablespoons of unsalted butter in a skillet. Stir in a handful of chopped walnuts and brown briefly. Add 2 tablespoons of runny honey and 2 tablespoons of scotch. Stir until heated through.

Vanilla ice-cream with Walnut and Honey Sauce

4 CHOCOLATE AND COFFEE SAUCE

Melt 2 tablespoons of unsalted butter in a saucepan. Add 3 ounces semisweet chocolate with 1 tablespoon of water and stir over a low heat until melted. Pour in 2 or 3 tablespoons of strong black coffee and 1 tablespoon of brandy. Sweeten to taste with a little confectioners' sugar.

5 CABINET SAUCES

Simply use either Raisins in Scotch or Prunes in Brandy (see page 19) spooned over the ice-cream.

Menu Suggestions

We have put together a range of menus which we hope will help the reader use the book to even greater effect. When planning these menus we obviously took into account a balance of tastes and textures, but we have also tried to make working in the kitchen as simple and as fast as possible. With this in mind, we have tried to ensure that the same cooking technique or piece of equipment is never used more than once in each menu.

For ease of reference, our menus are divided into four categories:

VERY FAST – where the whole meal may be cooked in *almost* 10 minutes

FORMAL – for very fast entertaining

INFORMAL – for very fast lunches and suppers

MEATLESS – for vegetarian and "demi-veg" meals (containing some fish, but no meat or poultry)

VERY FAST

Avocado, Spinach, and Lemon Soup, (*page 36*)
Pasta with Raw Egg, Parma Ham, and Chives (*page 45*)
Strawberries with Cointreau (*page 114*)

Pine Nut Soup (*page 36*)
Pasta with Fresh Tomatoes and Mint (*page 45*)
Salad with Pour-over Dressing (*page 57*)
Fruit and cheese

Mushrooms, Shallot, and Cream Eggs en Cocotte (*page 53*)
Chicken Livers with Orange (*page 96*)
Salad with Walnuts (*page 61*)
Fruit

Smoked Trout and Dill Eggs (*page 50*)
Salad with Avocado (*page 60*)
Fruit and cheese

Egg and Blue Cheese Salad (*page 67*)
Melon with Muscat (*page 114*)

FORMAL

Basic Eggs en Cocotte (*page 53*)
Noisettes of Lamb with Tomatoes (*page 97*)
Flageolets (*page 21*)
Fresh Fruit (*page 112*)

Five-spice Seared Salmon (*page 76*)
Snow Pea Noodles (*page 106*)
Salad with Avocado (*page 60*)
Peaches in Rosé Wine (*page 114*)

Creamy Corn Soup (*page 20*)
Chicken with Vermouth and Sage (*page 91*)
Rice with Pine Nuts (*page 109*)
Salad with Pour-over Dressing (*page 57*)
Cheese

Melon Salad (*page 62*)
Pan-fried Tuna with Fennel and Sun-dried Tomatoes (*page 75*)
Vanilla ice-cream with Chocolate and Coffee Sauce (*page 117*)

Chicken Wings with Marmalade (*page 90*)
Pasta with Fresh Tomatoes and Mint (*page 45*)
Salad with Anchovy Vinaigrette (*page 59*)
Peaches with Amaretti (*page 112*)

Watercress, Herb, and Cream Cheese Eggs en Cocotte (*page 53*)
Duck with Cranberry Sauce (*page 92*)
Rice with Bay Leaves (*page 109*)
Salad with Pour-over Dressing (*page 57*)
Fresh Fruit (*page 112*)

Jumbo Shrimp with Coriander (*page 80*)
Grilled steaks with Brandy and Pepper Butter (*page 101*)
Steam-boiled Vegetables (*page 104*)
Fruit Gratin (*page 113*)

Mushroom Salad (*page 68*)
Cornish Hen with Herbs and Olives (*page 90*)
Snow Pea Noodles (*page 106*)
Raspberry and Lemon Balm Fool (*page 115*)

INFORMAL

Herb Velouté (*page 37*)
Blood Sausage with Apple (*page 94*)
Ice-cream with Hot Marmalade Sauce (*page 117*)

Herb Hamburger (*page 100*)
Grilled Vegetables (*page 105*)
Vanilla ice-cream with Walnut and Honey Sauce (*page 117*)

Cauliflower Soup (*page 40*)
Chicken Liver and Chili Salad (*page 62*)
Pan-fried Apple Slices (*page 112*)

Bean and Tuna Salad (*page 21*)
Ham and Leek Stir-fried Eggs (*page 50*)
Steam-boiled Vegetables (*page 104*)
Fresh Fruit (*page 112*)

Leek Salad (*page 64*)
10-minute Stroganoff (*page 98*)
Basic Butter Noodles (*page 106*)
Frosted Fruit (*page 112*)

MEATLESS

Carrot and Lime Juice Salad (*page 64*)
Pasta with Walnut and Thyme (*page 45*)
Salad with Ripe Olives (*page 60*)
Fruit Skewers with Rum Butter (*pages 113 and 114*)
Lettuce and Pea Soup (*page 37*)
Zucchini, Tomato, and Thyme Eggah (*page 51*)
Salad with Parmesan (*page 61*)
Fresh Fruit (*page 112*)

Quick-marinated Smoked Haddock (*page 78*)
Pasta with Shredded Zucchini, Pine Nuts, and Tarragon (*page 47*)
Salad with Labna Balls (*page 18*)
Melon with Muscat (*page 114*)

Cucumber and Tarragon Soup (*page 36*)
Cod Steaks with Mustard (*page 78*)
Rice with Thyme (*page 109*)
Mango and Lime Fool (*page 115*)

Tomato Soup (*page 36*)
Grilled fish with Green Peppercorn Butter (*page 86*)
Salad with Cilantro and Parsley Dressing (*page 59*)
Baked Bananas (*page 113*)

Tarator (*page 36*)
Pasta with Anchovies, Capers, Parsley, and Thyme (*page 45*)
Salad with Ripe Olives (*page 60*)
Strawberries with Kirsch (*page 114*)

Index

For reasons of length, we have only been able to list occurrences of items as a principal ingredient.

Acknowledgments

The authors would like to express their thanks to:

Alaphia Bidwell, Anna del Conte, Peter Graham, Jack Lang, Heidi Lascelles, Patricia Lousada, Anne-Sophie Naudin, Sri Owen, and Yan-Kit So for kindly contributing recipes or allowing them to quote from their recipes.

Anne Furniss, Lewis Esson, Paul Welti, Jess Koppel, and Penny Mishcon for their help, encouragement, and patience.

Finally to the members of the Cinema Club for their constructive (and, at times, destructive) criticism.

The publishers would also like to thank Magimix for their cooperation in lending one of their Système Cuisine food processors for use in photography.

Editorial Direction: Lewis Esson
Publishing
Design: Paul Welti
Photography: Jess Koppel
Illustration: David Downton
Food for Photography: Meg Jansz
Styling: Penny Mishcon
American Editor: Norma MacMillan
Editorial Assistant: Penny David
Production: Sonya Sibbons